W9-AHS-699

Cooking – and Coping – Among the Cacti

Food and Nutrition in History and Anthropology
A series edited by Solomon H. Katz, University of Pennsylvania

This book is part of a series. The publisher will accept continuation orders which may be cancelled at any time and which provide for automatic billing and shipping of each title in the series upon publication. Please write for details.

Cooking – and Coping – Among the Cacti

Diet, Nutrition and Available Income in Northwestern Mexico

Roberta D. Baer

University of South Florida, Tampa

and

*Centro de Investigacion
en Alimentacion y Desarrollo
Hermosillo, Sonora, Mexico*

Gordon and Breach Publishers

Australia • Canada • China • France • Germany • India
Japan • Luxembourg • Malaysia • The Netherlands • Russia
Singapore • Switzerland • Thailand

TX
360
M4 B34
1998

c.1

39526990   9-9-99

Copyright © 1998 OPA (Overseas Publishers Association) Amsterdam B.V.
Published under license under the Gordon and Breach Publishers imprint.

All rights reserved.

No part of this book may be reproduced or utilized in any form or by any means, electronic or mechanical, including photocopying and recording, or by any information storage or retrieval system, without permission in writing from the publisher. Printed in India.

Amsteldijk 166
1st Floor
1079 LH Amsterdam
The Netherlands

Earlier versions of some of the material in this book have been published under different titles in: *Urban Anthropology*, vol. 16(1) (1987); *Food and Nutrition Bulletin*, vol. 12(4) (1990); *Human Dimensions of Food Policy*, Athens, Georgia: University of Georgia Press (1991); and *Social Science and Medicine*, vol. 36(3) (1993).

British Library Cataloguing in Publication Data

Baer, Roberta D.
   Cooking – and coping – among the cacti : diet, nutrition
   and available income in northwestern Mexico. – (Food and
   nutrition in history and anthropology : v. 13)
   1. Nutrition surveys – Mexico – Sonora   2. Food habits –
   Mexico – Sonora
   I. Title
   394.1'097217'09049

ISBN 90-5699-576-6

Printed and Bound at Ajanta Offset, New Delhi, India

Contents

Series Editor's Preface

The study of the origin, development and diversity of the human diet is emerging as a coherent field that offers a much-needed integrative framework for our contemporary knowledge of the ecology of food and nutrition. This authoritative series of monographs and symposia volumes on the history and anthropology of food and nutrition is designed to address this need by providing integrative approaches to the study of various problems within the human food chain. Since the series is both methodologically and conceptually integrative, the focus of the individual volumes spans such topics as nutrition and health, culinary practices, prehistoric analyses of diet, and food scarcity and subsistence practices among various societies of the world. As a series, it offers many unique opportunities for a wide range of scientists, scholars and other professionals representing anthropology, archaeology, food history, economics, agriculture, folklore, nutrition, medicine, pharmacology, public health and public policy to exchange important new knowledge, discoveries and methods involved in the study of all aspects of human foodways.

Solomon H. Katz

Acknowledgments

This research project was supported by a grant from the International Food Policy Research Institute, and I am grateful for the interest and assistance of Per Pinstrup-Andersen. Additional support was provided by grants from the Comins Fund of the University of Arizona, the Marwill Scholarship Fund, and the Tinker Foundation Summer Field Research Program. The ethnographic interview was originally developed as part of a project on food loss for the United States Department of Agriculture.

The help and support of my family and friends has been indispensable over the years. In addition, for their help in Hermosillo, I thank the entire staff of the Centro de Investigacíon en Alimentacíon y Desarrollo. While everyone was always most willing to offer their assistance with any types of problems I encountered, a few people deserve particular mention.

Carlos Peña, director of the Centro, encouraged my interest in being associated with the Centro; Mauro Valencia, head of the Department of Nutrition and Food Science, assisted in the analyses of the anthropometric data; Mario Guevara did the computer analyses of the anthropometric data; Pablo Wong developed the methodology used to deflate the income data; and Patricia Salido helped me make sense of the "legalese" of many of the land documents, and always seemed to know which office to try next to find the missing data.

Mario Camberos generously permitted me to work with the raw data from his study of the labor force in Hermosillo; Patricia Jardines spent long hours helping me assign codes to foods; Marta Peña, Flor Dominguez and Hortensia Gonzales did a great deal of coding for me; and I appreciate Kathy Denman's interest in promoting anthropology at C.I.A.D. Thanks also to Enrique and Lucia Ramos for their friendship, support and interest in my work.

The encouragement of Cynthia Radding Murrieta and others at I.N.A.H. in Hermosillo is gratefully acknowledged. For their tolerance of my never-ending stream of queries about anything and everything connected with food, as well as their hospitality, I thank the three families with whom I lived: the Arandas, the Galvezes and the Limones. Without Leita Curran's advice on finding an auto mechanic, the entire project would have ground to an untimely halt on numerous occasions.

My work in Arroyo Lindo and the neighboring villages was greatly facilitated by the cooperation I received from local officials, school teachers, health personnel and the people of Arroyo Lindo, Los Cerritos and Milpas Verdes. Marta Borquez helped as a field assistant in Arroyo Lindo, and with her help and that of Osvaldo Landavaso, I was able to find all the migrants in Hermosillo. Many government offices in Hermosillo permitted me access to their archives; their courtesy and assistance were much appreciated.

Special thanks to the 105 women and their families who so kindly submitted to my endless questions about how many teaspoons of sugar went into each person's coffee, and so on. Their cooperation and kindness made it all so much easier.

In Tucson, many faculty and friends made my graduate career and the writing of the dissertation on which this book is based less stressful. Clyde Feldman and Roberta Hagarman were most generous in helping me with the mysteries of the computer, and Rhonda Dixon assisted often with last-minute typing. Wilson Hughes and the Garbage Project provided all kinds of back-up support.

The members of my dissertation committee – Cheryl Ritenbaugh, Gail Harrison, Bill Rathje and Carlos Velez-Ibanez – were most helpful in their support of my work. I also thank a number of people who read and commented on earlier versions of parts of this book: Pat Culbert, Bob Netting, Michael Schiffer, Barbara Babcock, Ted Downing, Ellen Messer, Jim Bindon and Gene Anderson.

In the process of revisions that have led to this book, I note the help and encouragement of my friends and colleagues at the University of South Florida, in particular Mike Angrosino for his editorial suggestions, and Jeannine Coreil for her support of this endeavor. Many graduate students at USF, among them Marcela Gutierrez-Mayka and Karen Smith, assisted over the years in re-analyses of the original data. Marianne Bell and Carole Rennick typed many of the tables.

Finally, the support over the years of my Council on Nutritional Anthropology colleagues has also been important. I thank Sol Katz, who made a number of helpful suggestions, and Rebecca Huss-Ashmore, who offered critical advice during the process of final review and revisions.

CHAPTER 1

The Basic Recipe
An Introduction

The setting for this book is the northwest of Mexico, a desert land of dry mountain ranges and saguaro cacti. It is a landscape familiar from Western films. This book focuses on life in several small villages outside of Hermosillo, the capital of the state of Sonora, as well as in that city itself. This area is one of great contrasts between old and new, between some of the most modern agriculture in the world and some of the most traditional. There is great wealth and prosperity, both in the cities as well as the villages. But in both areas, stunted malnourished children can be observed, in numbers which seem unusual given the level of development in this part of Mexico.

My goal in choosing this area to study was to try to understand the people of this region and their customs, as well as why these contrasts existed. The method used was an in-depth nutritional anthropological study of all aspects of people's lives that might relate to their daily diets, as well as a detailed analysis of those diets themselves. Nutritional anthropology is the study of socio-cultural aspects of food consumption and nutritional status. The goal of this book is to demonstrate the kind of data analysis used in nutritional anthropology, as well as the policy recommendations which can result from such research.

The key questions of the research were:

1) Why was malnutrition observed in this setting?
2) What would be needed to improve diets for the malnourished – i.e., was there a lack of income in those households, did the mothers of these children need more nutritional education, or what other kinds of changes and/or programs and/or government policies would ameliorate the nutritional problems?

This approach to answering these questions combines qualitative methods (detailed ethnographic and archival research, without which it is impossible to understand land tenure problems, for example) with quantitative analyses of income, diet, and nutritional status. The result is a model for understanding behavior at the household level that affects dietary patterns, based on a new analytic concept, "available income." This model of analysis is applied to the Sonoran data to make it possible to understand why people eat what they do, why they make the choices they do, and to develop policy recommendations to affect these patterns. As such, this research combines both in-depth ethnography and quantitative analysis to address an applied problem in a specific locale. But the model of analysis presented here is not locale specific and is appropriate for application in other areas of the world to solve recurrent problems of nutrition outreach.

Relationships between increases in household income and improvements in diet and nutritional status have not proven to be as linear as was once expected (Berg 1973). This book, nevertheless, accepts the importance of income as a key factor in predicting dietary patterns. It does so from the perspective of allocation of household cash income, or how income is used, with particular interest in expenditures for food. But whereas traditional studies have focused on total household income, or on the total sum of the money earned by all the employed members of the household, I prefer to focus on a variable I call "available income," which refers to the amount of money that is actually available to those in the household responsible for household expenditures, including food. Available income is not, however, the same as "total food expenditure." On the contrary, it represents the total sum that is available to those who make decisions about all household expenditures, of which expenditures for food are but one part – a part, moreover, that often has to compete with other wants and needs.

The concept seems almost too simplistic. Surely this conclusion is, and has been self-evident for some time now. But household income and/or total food expenditure remain the common foci of analysis. I cannot even claim to have invented the concept of "available income." The phenomenon was pointed out to me by a woman in rural Mexico with a third grade education. When asked about the amount of money her 18 year old daughter made, she responded, "Do you want to know how much she makes, or how much she gives me?"

The great value of the concept of "available income" is that it is affected by a variety of social and cultural variables, such as residential patterns, home production of food, and the extent to which women are employed outside the home. It thus incorporates the effects of these variables and provides a way of understanding the network of socio-cultural factors affecting food consumption patterns. Yet it does so without reducing or simplifying the complexity of the social web. The focus shifts to an understanding of how households with similar total income may come to have different amounts of available income. But even households of similar available incomes may differ in their food expenditures and consumption, due to other social and cultural variables, such as ethnicity, nutritional knowledge, and desires for consumer goods, all of which affect allocation of available income. The remainder of this chapter discusses the aspects of people's lives that are responsible for variations in available income and in differing patterns of food consumption in households of similar total household incomes.

DETERMINATION OF AVAILABLE INCOME

There is no question that income and relative prices are of prime importance in determining the food consumption patterns of a household (Berg 1973; Au Coin *et al.*, 1972; Greiner and Latham 1981). Income may come into a household, or into the hands of a member of that household, but there is no guarantee that those funds will be used for food purchases. How much money is really available to those responsible for household expenditures (including food)? How is this money allocated among competing wants and needs? The amount of available income will be affected by the extent to which wage-earners in each household make all, a portion, or none of their earnings available to those making household expenditures. The concept of available income is not related to who makes the decision as to how the income is to be spent; it merely refers to the sum of money about which decisions about household expenditures are made by those in the household responsible for such decisions.

Much of the research on income allocation in relation to food consumption has focused on the particular importance of women's earnings. Women's incomes tend to be less seasonal than those of men, and in many parts of the world women retain complete control over their earnings. In studies in West Africa (Dwyer 1983; Guyer 1980; Tripp 1982), and Kerala, India (Kumar 1978), increases in women's incomes have been associated with improvements in food consumption and/or nutritional status. Women tend to spend their incomes on food or other household necessities, thus raising available income.

Some studies, however, suggest that patterns of income allocation based on household role may be more important than those of gender in their effects on food consumption patterns. It would be expected, for example, that a wife's economic activity would have a greater impact on the amount of available income than would that of a grown child who may only give a portion (or none) of his/her earnings to his/her parents. The extent to which most members of a household retain control over their incomes, and dispose of them as they see fit, has been pointed out. For example, Whitehead notes than in the area of northeastern Ghana she studied, "virtually all men, women, and children over 10 have some form of money income" (1981:94). Further, two-thirds of the households consist of between five and twenty adults, and "no other person has rights over an individual's cash income" (Whitehead 1981:100). Data from Mexico City show a similar pattern. In that situation, there was no general pattern of the extent to which grown children contributed to household expenses; the mother's ability to convince her children to contribute and the economic situation of the particular household seemed to be the key variables. In general, the children contributed, at most, only a portion of their earnings (Beneria and Roldan 1987).

The amount of available income will also be affected by the extent to which a household produces some of the food it consumes, thus decreasing out of pocket expenditures for food. Much of the pattern of declines in nutritional status associated in some studies with the shift from subsistence to market production (Fleuret and Fleuret 1980) is probably due to declining available income. Households cannot afford to buy back the quality of diet they once produced for themselves. Even small amounts of home production (as from a family garden) can have significant positive impact on food consumption (Smith *et al.* 1983), because the available income of the household is increased.

ALLOCATION OF AVAILABLE INCOME

Patterns of allocation of available income will be affected by a number of other variables. Increased economic activity of women may increase the amounts of money over which they have control, and/or their roles in household decision making with regard to expenditures. The extent to which this increased influence actually translates into dietary changes may be related to nutritional knowledge of the wife, as well as to relative desires for prestige foods and consumer goods.

Nutritional knowledge may be an important variable; even if low income is a constraint, a more adequate diet can in many cases be obtained by better utilization of actual resources. Traditional diets were the result of centuries of cultural knowledge about what foods to consume and how to combine them. The transition from subsistence to market economies has supplied most contemporary Third World societies with many new foods. The house-hold is left in the position of having unfamiliar foods from which to select, without any cultural guidelines to use in making this selection. The situation can be further worsened by the role of advertising which seeks to promote the new foods, often convincing low income households that consumption of high priced products is necessary for good nutrition (Berg 1972).

Prestige values of particular foods may cause changes in food consumption patterns, particularly the rejection of low prestige foods (Devadas 1970; Cussler and de Give 1942), which are usually associated with the poor. Such foods include sweet potatoes in the U.S. South (Fitzgerald 1976), bean curd in Hong Kong (Anderson and Anderson 1977), and wild greens in Mexico (Messer 1976). Often, however, prestige foods may not be as nutritious as those which they replace (McKenzie 1974; Burgess and Dean 1962; Read 1964; den Hartog and Bornstein-Johansson 1976), though in most instances they are more expensive (Berg 1972).

Consumer goods may also compete for available income since income is often used to purchase them in an attempt to garner prestige (Marchione 1980). Such prestige items include clothing, radios, and bicycles (den Hartog and Bornstein-Johansson 1976). The importance of certain types of consumer goods as symbols of prestige should not be underestimated. Simic (1973) reported that rural Yugoslavian villagers often bought radios and displayed them prominently as prestige items – despite the fact that their homes lacked the electricity necessary to make the radios work.

ROLE OF ETHNICITY

Another variable of importance in affecting both the amount of available income, and the manner in which available income is allocated, is ethnicity.

The amount of available income will be affected by ethnic patterns of income control and allocation of men and women, as well as by ethnic household residential patterns, e.g., the extent to which working adults who are not members of the same nuclear family reside together (and pool or separate incomes). Residential patterns may also mitigate the sometimes cited negative effects on household nutrition of women's work, due to the reduced time women have available for cooking and childcare (Popkin and Solon 1976); it may be possible to depend on other household members for help with these activities.

Allocation of available income will be affected by ethnicity through effects of culture specific norms about the roles of men and women in decision-making; some cultures limit women's input in decision making, while others encourage it. Ethnic background will also be important in terms of traditional food choices, and the relative importance of the foods that the larger society defines as being of high prestige value. Ethnic groups trying to assimilate into the larger society may strive to emulate the eating habits of those they perceive to be more mainstream. Eskimo diets, for example, presently include such items as soft drinks, crackers, and potato chips (Kemp 1971). Groups trying to maintain distinct identities may deliberately avoid the foods of the larger society and choose another outside reference group whose food habits to emulate. For example, the Hokkien Chinese in Malaysia, who seek to differentiate themselves from the Malaysians, avoid Malay foods, while using those foods that they associate with the higher prestige western societies (Anderson and Anderson 1977).

OTHER VARIABLES

Two other variables are often cited in the literature as affecting dietary patterns. The first of these, rural to urban migration, can be viewed as an extension of a change in subsistence pattern, and would be expected to reflect similar types of effects on available income.

The second variable, intra-household distribution of food, may also be suggested as being related to available income, i.e., it could be predicted that in larger households with more workers, differences between available income and household income would be greater than in smaller households. Reduced available income, and consequent decreases in food purchases, might be an alternative explanation for the nutritional problems seen in larger households to that of unequal distribution of food among members of those households, as has been suggested in some studies (e.g., Whiteford 1982).

THE CASE STUDY – SONORA OF THE EARLY 1980's

These variables are investigated using data collected between 1981 and 1984 in Sonora, a state in northwestern Mexico. Though a decade has now passed since the data were collected, no attempt has been made to update the ethnographic data, which are presented in the ethnographic present. As a case study illustrating the use of the available income model, the particular age of the data used is not important. Moreover, the book is more than just an illustration of the utility of the concept of available income. That analysis is based on a detailed ethnographic examination of the complexity of income, belief, diet, and health in a specific location. In the early 1980's, both urban and rural northwestern Mexico were thoroughly integrated into the market economy. Mexico has changed greatly since then, due to NAFTA, the changes in land tenure law, as well as the devaluations of the peso in 1994–5. The ethnographic data presented here thus represent a baseline that can be used to assess the effects of these more recent economic and social changes. In other areas of Mexico, these kinds of analyses will be more difficult, as there are no such baseline data and/or, in addition to the more recent changes, the areas may not have previously been a part of the market economy.

SUMMARY

This book presents a model for understanding relationships between dietary patterns and income. Dietary, anthropometric, ethnographic, and archival data from Northwestern Mexico are used to illustrate the importance and utility of the available income model. The roles of other variables associated with dietary patterns are examined, as well as their effects on and the way they are effected by available income. The variables under consideration include income, subsistence pattern, prestige, desires for consumer goods, ethnicity, women's roles, intra-household distribution of food, rural versus urban residence, and nutritional knowledge. This process will demonstrate the extent to which available income is a critical variable in understanding dietary patterns, and in designing and evaluating effective food policies and programs.

CHAPTER 2

The Critical Ingredients
The Ethnographic Context

OVERVIEW OF SONORA

The state of Sonora is located in the extreme northwestern part of Mexico (see Figures 1 and 2). Its great distance from Mexico City and the population concentrations in the central part of Mexico, as well as

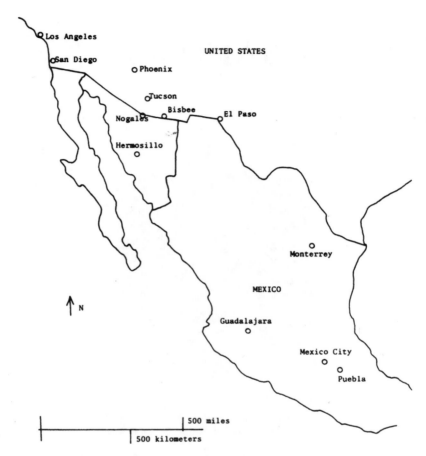

Figure 1. Sonora in the Context of the United States and Mexico.

its proximity to large population centers in the United States – Tucson and Phoenix – have played an important role in the development of the regional style and culture of Sonora. This culture has been described (Ruiz: personal communication) as reflecting the ambivalent love-hate attitude that Sonorans have with "el otro lado" (the other side), as the United States is described. Relationships between Sonora and "el otro lado" not only have cultural aspects, but are also geographical, historical, ecological, and economic. In addition to this ambivalent stance with regard to the north, Sonorans also have a somewhat ambivalent attitude as they look to the south. Sonora has always been ranching country and this,

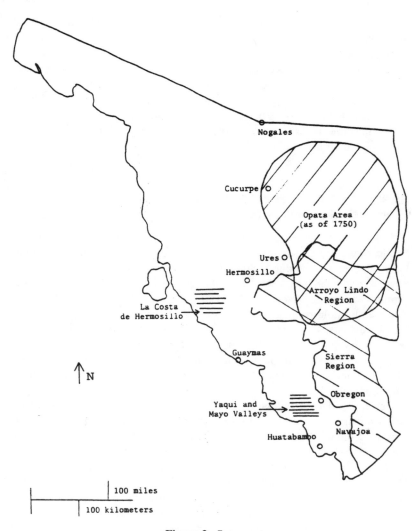

Figure 2. Sonora.

as well as its location on the extreme frontier, has lead to a regional style
that stresses independence. Sonorans view themselves as Sonorans first,
and only then as Mexicans. Mexicans from other areas are referred to as
"guachos," a mildly derogatory term. As such, a Sonoran culture has
developed which combines aspects of both Mexican and North American
cultures in a distinctly Sonoran way.

Sonora is largely a desert and arid mountain environment, characterized by scrub vegetation and the "classic" saguaro cactus. The economy of the state is primarily based on cattle ranching, with both cheese and beef being produced. Intensive, highly capitalized agriculture is practiced as well, as is chicken and egg production. Other sources of employment include mining (largely open pit mines), and fishing. Very little subsistence agriculture is carried out, and as such, almost all households are integrated into the market economy, either by participation in wage labor or by involvement in commercial agriculture and/or ranching.

EARLIER STUDIES IN MESTIZO SONORA: ETHNOGRAPHIC STUDIES

Anthropologists have not been drawn in any great numbers to Sonora. While research has been carried out in the Indian communities, particularly the Yaqui of southern Sonora, the mestizo villages and cities in the area formerly inhabited by the Opata Indians have been largely ignored. These areas represent the antithesis of the type of places on which traditional anthropology focused, having neither numerous colorful fiestas nor exotic customs. Further, the villages are not isolated entities, but are very much in psychological touch with, and have physical ties to the larger culture of Sonora, and through that, with those of the United States and Mexico. These ties affect all Sonorans, even if they live in rural areas from which they themselves do not travel extensively.

Hewes conducted fieldwork in 1931 in a village north of Ures, which had an irrigation system. Village agriculture was important, and crops produced included wheat, corn, beans, chile, sugarcane, tobacco, squash, watermelons, onions, and sweet potatoes. Chickens were raised, as well as cattle, the latter producing milk (some of which was made into cheese). However, cattle raising was hampered by insufficient pasture and water. Nevertheless, the village was largely self-sufficient. Occasional agricultural surpluses were sold, as were cattle, cheese and dried beef (*carne machaca*). The cash was used to purchase clothing, furniture, gas and potatoes (Hewes 1935).

Owen (1959) studied a village on the western edge of the former Opata region. He noted that there was a great deal of travel to the United States (and very little to the Mexican cities to the south.) "Such names as Tucson, Bisbee, Phoenix and Los Angeles are more familiar to the villagers than are the names of Mexico's major cities" (Owen 1959:21). Attitudes seemed to follow experiences: the United States was viewed favorably, while non-Sonoran Mexicans were generally disliked.

Exposure to the United States led to a group awareness of modern agricultural methods, but most people in the village were too poor to use other than traditional agricultural approaches. Food was not grown for household use; much of the harvest was sold for cash and staples were later purchased as they were needed. In addition to agricultural products, cattle were raised. However, the arid nature of this region made ranching, as well as farming, often quite risky. Even a slight change in the rainfall was often enough to change the balance from sufficient forage to starvation for the animals (Owen 1959).

Animals were butchered about twice a month, and the owner of the animal distributed meat to those who helped him, as well as to other kin, and to his household. The remainder was sold to other people in the village. In addition to meat, other common foods consumed were beans, boiled or fried potatoes, flour and corn tortillas, eggs, coffee, seasonal vegetables, and soft drinks. There was very little hunting. Among the gathered foods were *chiltepin* (a small chile) and greens, though use of gathered food was greater among the poorer segments of the population.

Sheridan (1983) studied Cucurpe, on the northwestern edge of the Opata area. This village has a mixed economy of farming and ranching. While the nature of the range will not support cattle on natural pasture alone, Cucurpe's irrigation system allows the shortfall in cattle fodder to be planted, as well as permitting some subsistence production. Hunting and gathering are also sources of food. Important other factors in this economy are the credit and assistance that have been received through government programs, as well as the remittances sent by those who have emigrated from Cucurpe. Also important for community leadership have been the skills brought back by returning emigrants.

Thus, while there has not been a great deal of anthropological work done in the mestizo villages of eastern-central Sonora, it is possible to see some general patterns and characteristics of the area. With regard to urban Sonora, there is even less background available. Erasmus (1961) does provide some information on Navajoa and Huatabambo, towns in southern Sonora; he estimates that the middle and upper classes may have represented between a fourth and a third of the population. The middle class had grown considerably (in absolute numbers) over the previous decade.

Social mobility also increased during that period, with an increase in buying the consumer goods that were the principal symbols of status. Much of this buying was done either by or for the unmarried women in the family, some of whom were working and helping to make the payments on the newly acquired goods. "Often families competing in this new conspicuous ownership race try to save money by subsisting on the peasant diet of tortillas and beans. On several occasions I heard people jokingly depreciate the household improvements of another family with the comment, 'but they do not eat'" (Erasmus 1961:243).

While there was much class consciousness, there was also a high value placed on social equality. "...In contrast to the country people, who always stress the equality of poverty, the townspeople put great emphasis on the equality of opportunity" (Erasmus 1961:240). A kind of Horatio Alger-like ethic seemed to prevail, although there was something of a discrepancy between the ideal and the reality. Generally, however, a "Protestant ethic" of "work hard and don't waste money and you will succeed" seemed to have taken hold in this strongly Roman Catholic environment. The upwardly mobile middle class had a strong concern for the education of its children. This attitude was also becoming common among the better-off rural families, who often moved to the towns so that their children could further their education.

STUDIES OF ECONOMIC DEVELOPMENT AND NUTRITIONAL STATUS

This expansion of the middle class in southern Sonora was due in part to government sponsored irrigation projects in the Yaqui and Mayo valleys. These projects, and other investment in agriculture were generally directed toward areas of large-scale privately owned lands. This strategy represented a shift at the national level from the extensive expansion reform programs of the thirties (Arizpe 1981). The focus on large scale irrigation agriculture has led on the national level to an increase in income concentration, which the government has encouraged as a way of generating funds for investment (Barkin 1975).

Agricultural development in Sonora has followed this pattern, and to a certain extent, is held up as an example of its success (Silvers and Crossen 1980). The most recent example of this type of development has taken place on "La Costa de Hermosillo," located to the west of that city. There sophisticated irrigation agriculture produces wheat, alfalfa, cotton, grapes, citrus fruit, and nuts, a good part of which is for export. Irrigation is necessary because given the arid climate of Sonora, large scale rain-fed agriculture is nearly impossible. The prosperity observed by Erasmus (1961) in southern Sonora, and that which is seen today in Hermosillo, are partially the result of these development projects.

However, this prosperity and accumulation of wealth in some parts of the state have been achieved at the expense of other areas, in particular, the Sierra region.

It was necessary for the success of the irrigation and growth projects in the coastal valleys to minimize division of the headwaters of the Sonoran rivers – that is, to discourage the development of more marginal lands in eastern Sonora in favor of more productive development of the rich coastal bottomlands. This, in part, explains the lack of credit to the Sierra ejidos, and the decision not to extend the small irrigation program to the Sonoran Sierra where it would result in less water for...more prestigious projects (Sanderson 1981:20–1).

The term "productive development," however, must be interpreted in terms of the national priorities of development, which favor market versus subsistence production. This pattern began in the late 30's and was maintained in later development projects in Sonora. "By 1979, the capitalization of agriculture in Sonora had produced a remarkable dualism, characterized by a few highly technological, costly irrigation districts producing crops for export, and the rest of the state remaining relatively valueless, producing at best for self consumption" (Sanderson 1981:152). Given this pattern of investment, the economic miracle of Sonora may not be that the irrigated areas produce so much, but rather that those in the Sierra produce anything at all, given the lack of aid that has been made available to them (Sanderson 1981).

This pattern of "development," or lack thereof in the Sierra region, has led to large scale migration from this region. Thus, some of the most important resources of the Sierra – labor and water – have been transferred to other areas of the state, creating a classic example of the development of under-development.

In the context of this type of economic development, the finding of significant levels of mild to moderate malnutrition in both the economically marginally rural and urban areas of the state is not surprising. Anthropometric data from nutrition surveys conducted in the early 1980's indicated that the highest rates of malnutrition are found in school-age children (5 to 14 years), with the most serious problems seen in the urban areas (Valencia 1980; 1981). These nutritional studies also provide important demographic data, such as the finding that lower income urban households are, in a large part, made up of rural-born husbands and urban-born wives. Average household size in the urban areas sampled was 5.8 persons (Valencia 1981), as opposed to that of the rural areas of 6.5 persons (Valencia 1980).

STUDY POPULATIONS

Four populations were sampled: (1) Households in Arroyo Lindo (a pseudonym, as are all names of villages and individuals), a rural village located in the Sierra region of Sonora, which was characterized by significant levels of mild to moderate malnutrition, as well as a high degree of out-migration (20 households, 156 individuals) (2) Households in which both heads of household (this refers to the husband and wife in each household) were raised in Arroyo Lindo or a nearby village, and who had migrated to the state capital of Hermosillo (20 households, 129 individuals) (3) Households in which both household heads were born (or raised from a very early age) in Hermosillo (38 households, 229 individuals) (4) Households in which the wife was American and in which the entire family (wife, husband, and children) was living permanently in Hermosillo (27 households, 126 individuals). The backgrounds of the wives were both Anglo-American (i.e., U.S. citizens of non-Mexican ancestry) and Mexican–American, but in all cases, the women considered their nationality to be American.

These sample groups are hereafter referred to as: rural residents, migrants, born in the city, and Americans (see Tables 1, 2, 3). Due to differing sizes of the sample groups, in analyses which cross-cut these groups, the data were weighted as follows:

Arroyo Lindo – 1.32
Migrants – 1.32
Born in the city – 0.66

The Americans were only included in the analyses of the role of ethnicity in Chapter 4.

To insure similarity of household type, in the first three sample groups, each household sampled had both male and female heads (i.e., husband and wife) and at least two children. In addition, no household in which any woman was more than four months pregnant or lactating was included, to avoid individuals whose nutritional needs would be hard to quantify. In the

Table 1. The Sampling Plan: Number of Households

	Arroyo Lindo	Migrants	Urban Born	Americans
Economically Active Wife				
Low Income	8	7	3	0
Middle Income	3	3	9	14
Non-Economically Active Wife				
Low Income	7	2	15	1
Middle Income	2	8	11	12
Totals	20	20	38	27

Table 2. Incomes of Sample Households

	Lower Income		Higher Income	
	Number	%	Number	%
Arroyo Lindo N = 20	15	75	5	25
Migrants N = 20	9	4	11	55
Urban Born N = 38	18	47	20	53
Americans N = 27	1	4	26	96

Per Capita. Income Categories: Lower Income 0–$49,000;
Higher Income over $49,001.
(In pesos: 40 pesos = $1.00).

Table 3. Mean Annual Per Capita Household Income*

Group	Mean Income
Arroyo Lindo	39,031
Migrants	58,669
Urban Born	54,538
p	<0.0001

*(In pesos: 40 pesos = $1.00).

case of the Americans, because of the small size of the population, households with one child and/or a pregnant or lactating wife were included, but no dietary data on pregnant or lactating women were used in calculating group means.

Moreover, in each group sampled, it was planned to have half of the sample be of households where the wife was economically active. "Economic activity" was defined as either receiving a separate paycheck, or contributing labor for work (in addition to housework) for which a paycheck was not received, as in work in family businesses. The use of this term is not meant to imply that women who engage in other types of unremunerated household work are not also economically productive. But for the purposes of this volume, the term "economically active" does serve to describe the role of the women who were involved in activities in addition to housework, without resort to even more unwieldly terminology, such as "women engaged in remunerated activities."

Each sample group is representative of a wide range of incomes; however some adjustments had to be made to the income data, as they were
collected during 1982. This was a period of economic chaos in Mexico,
which included three devaluations of the peso. Such times of economic
turmoil are not uncommon in Mexico. The events of late 1994 and early
1995 may ultimately prove to have been an economic crisis of similar
magnitude to that of 1982 and the years following, and may be only the
first of many such crises. Thus, the data presented here, as well as the
methods used to collect and analyze those data can be seen to be of continued relevance, in the present, and perhaps on into the future. To deal with
the devaluations of 1982, a methodology of "income deflation" was utilized so that all of the data on household economics, though collected at
different times during the year, would be comparable. For some of the
analyses the groups were divided into lower (less than or equal to 49,000
pesos) and higher (greater than 49,000 pesos) income groupings of per
capita annual income. The value of the peso at the time of the study was
equal to U.S. $0.025.

Strategies used for selecting households to be included in the study varied slightly among the populations sampled. The most practical way of
finding Arroyo Lindo households of the desired type (in which one of the
household heads had a sibling married to another person from Arroyo
Lindo, both of whom had migrated to Hermosillo), was to seek referrals
from informants of different families who lived in different areas of the
village. The drawing of the migrant subsample was thus done in the course
of the selection of the rural subsample; members of the rural households
provided the addresses of their relatives in Hermosillo.

Selection of the urban born subsample was more problematic, as most
urban residents were migrants. Households with both heads born in the
city were therefore rare. As such, a system of using networks (very similar
to the strategy used in Arroyo Lindo) was employed. People who had been
born in Hermosillo were asked to suggest families that met the sample criteria. A number of different networks in different areas of the city, and
from different income strata were employed. In the case of the Americans,
a network strategy was also used to locate all of the members of this small
community who met the general sampling criteria. As such, unlike the
samples from the other populations, the conclusions about the Americans
can be extended to the entire community. On the basis of having lived and
interacted with the other three populations for a period of one year, I feel
that each group can be considered to be representative of the population
from which it was drawn. However, the urban-born subsample is representative only of households in which both households are urban-born, not of
urban households in general. The migrant households sampled are also

representative only of households in which both household heads are originally from the Arroyo Lindo region.

ASPECTS OF SAMPLE GROUPS: ARROYO LINDO

Arroyo Lindo, in many ways, is as typically Sonoran as any village could be. Originally Opata Indian, there is today no identification with this identity, although a few traits, such as the *fariseos* of Semana Santa (the young men of the village disguise themselves and dress in old clothes) still remain. Numerous families in Arroyo Lindo have relatives living in the United States, and a number of the men in the village worked in the United States when they were youths, often as an adventure. Many aspects of daily life are also typical of rural Sonora, showing extensive links not only with the larger Sonoran world, but also with those of "el otro lado." These were clear from the first moments of my arrival in the village:

"On the recommendation of Juan (who is from Arroyo Lindo), who I met through Miguel, upon arriving in the village I asked some friends of his if they could rent me a room. They (Elena and Mario) are quite nice, so for now I will be living there. We had coffee, chatted a bit, and then went off to visit Mario's mother in Milpas Verdes. It's a lovely small pueblo. His mother was making corn tortillas (with a little flour mixed in). I was offered coffee and then *cena* (a light evening meal). I ate with the grandfather, a thin old man who told me stories about how as a young man he traveled all over Sonora on his horse. He followed these with a discussion of the recent devaluation of the peso, its current value relative to the dollar, and how this affects everyone's ability to continue buying American clothing (these are either brought by traders, or people from here go shopping in the border towns). After *cena*, which turned out to be a soup of cabbage and soup bone served with corn and two kinds of flour tortillas, beans, homemade cheese, and orange soda, we retired to watch Bonanza re-runs on the television, which were interspersed with commercials for the V.H., the most expensive supermarket chain in Hermosillo. We returned home to Arroyo Lindo, and my first day in "THE FIELD" ended as I fell asleep to the sound of MASH re-runs on the family T.V." (Field Notes, March 1982).

"I stopped by today to see Juana. Her family is the poorest in the Arroyo Lindo sample, and all of her children are first degree malnourished. She commented that she really would have preferred for her daughter to study computer related work (I think she meant keypunching) instead of becoming a teacher" (Field notes, May 1982).

"Got back to the house very late, after stopping next door for a bowl of posole. I was really tired and wanted to go to bed, but Sandra, the trader, had the bed covered with American clothes she'd brought from the border to sell – and the

room was packed with people looking at them. So I dragged my sleeping bag
into the other room and slept on the couch" (Field notes, May 1982).

There are things about Arroyo Lindo that initially seem incongruous;
it is not the type of place where one would expect to find as many nutritional problems as were indicated by the nutritional surveys of the early
1980's (Valencia 1980; 1981). Arroyo Lindo is a relatively large village
(1713 inhabitants [Estado de Sonora 1980]), but its population has not grown
greatly in recent years, due to extensive migration. The out-migration is of
two types – that of adults, and that of children who are sent to Hermosillo
for advanced schooling (until 1976 there was no secondary school in
Arroyo Lindo). Return migration is not great, and is particularly rare
among the latter group. Among the former group, many return migrants
tend to be couples whose children have grown up, married, and remained
in the city.

Located on the highway (paved in 1974), Arroyo Lindo appears to be a
modern village that has received many government sponsored improvements, including morning and afternoon primary schools (1944), a secondary technical school (1976), evening adult literacy programs, a kindergarten
(1982), electricity for 95% of the population (1971) and running water
(1963). The quality of the water, however, is deficient. The water tank has
not been cleaned in 5 years, and the well is located in the lowest part of the
village (Chavez 1981). Further contamination of the water table is caused by
the use of several old wells as septic tanks. It has been recommended that
the water be chlorinated to be fit for use (Soto 1982). Many of the women
realize that the water should be boiled; they justify not doing so by noting
the way the children casually drink from any hose. What's the point of boiling the water at home, they say, when the kids will drink unboiled water
when they're not at home? Not unexpectedly, intestinal parasites are among
the most common medical problems (Soto 1982).

Arroyo Lindo also has street lights (1980), garbage collection (1981),
and a modern health center (1973) with a full-time doctor (completing
the required year of social service). Services available within the village
include: a new municipal office building and plaza, two churches (one
Catholic, one Protestant), a gas station, about 30 *tiendas* (small stores), a
general store, a tortilla factory, a municipal slaughterhouse, a bar, a hotel,
two restaurants, two establishments that sell beer, a drug store, a recreation
hall, playing fields, two car mechanics, a tire repairer, a saddle maker, a
shoemaker and three seamstresses. In addition to locally made clothes, villagers spend large amounts of money on ready-made clothing, and it is not
uncommon to see a person wearing a pair of designer jeans walking down
one of the unpaved streets of the village.

However, despite the modern amenities in Arroyo Lindo, the 1979 nutritional survey revealed relatively higher rates of malnutrition than would be expected in a state like Sonora (Table 4). Further, these nutritional problems did not seem to be the only type of local problem. Changes in the subsistence pattern and the type of development characteristic of Sonora during past decades have intensified other village problems.

Arroyo Lindo, traditionally a village of subsistence farmers and ranchers (primarily raising dairy cattle for the making of cheese), has over the past 30 to 40 years been integrated into the market economy. There is little irrigated land (74 out of the 1,318 hectares which are devoted to agriculture) (LERES 1979), and land that was previously planted with corn,

Table 4. Anthropometric Data for I.I.E.S.N.O. Sample in Arroyo Lindo*

		Less Than 1 yr. N = 21		1–4 yrs. N = 46		5–14 yrs. N = 54	
		Number	%	Number	%	Number	%
Height for Age							
Good Growth	>95%**	19	90	34	74	46	85
Poor Growth	<95%	2	10	12	26	8	15
Weight for Age							
Obese	>110%	3	14	7	15	2	4
Normal	90–110%	12	57	22	48	18	33
1st Degree Malnutrition	75–90%	4	19	11	24	27	50
2nd Degree Malnutrition	<60–75%	1	5	4	9	7	13
3rd Degree Malnutrition	<60%	1	5	2	4	0	0
Weight for Height							
Obese	>110%	4	19	5	11	3	6
Normal	90–110%	12	57	34	74	38	70
Mild Nutrition	85–90%	3	14	4	9	5	9
Moderate Malnutrition	75–85%	2	10	2	4	7	13
Severe Malnutrition	<75%	0	0	1	2	1	2

(Valencia: Personal Communication).
Note: These data were collected as part of a larger sample and are statistically valid only at the level of the total sample.
**Reference values are the Ramos Galvan median values in the appropriate age, sex, and measurement categories, based on the Mexican population (Ramos Galvan 1975).

wheat and some vegetables for home use is now planted with cattle fodder. Households owning cattle usually have a home in the village, as well as a ranch outside of the village where their cows are kept. Several relatives may keep their animals at the same ranch. One family lives at the ranch; usually it is a family without school age children, as it is difficult for children who live on ranches to get to the school in the village. Other members of the family go out to the ranch daily to care for their animals. The milk is made into cheese at the ranches and is generally sold directly from the ranches to traders who take it to Hermosillo. This cheese – *queso regional* – is an uncooked cheese, similar to cottage cheese. It is usually aged just overnight until most of the whey (which is fed to pigs) has drained off. The daily sale of cheese represents the bulk of most ranching families' incomes. Thus, even those whose families who have land and cattle do not commonly consume their own milk or cheese in their houses in the village.

Cattle used to be more commonly slaughtered in the village, and the owner of the animal gave the meat to friends and relatives. Now, as the selling price is higher in Hermosillo, those who can try to sell their animals there. It is also likely that, over time, the type of cattle slaughtered locally has changed. Cows that can no longer be milked are now the only cattle which are slaughtered; steers are sold at a very young age to larger ranchers. The availability of meat is uncertain and so obtaining it, as well as many other foods, is often a matter of keeping one's ear to the ground and knowing who is slaughtering, as well as who is selling what and where.

Today most of the food that is consumed is store bought, with the exception of flour tortillas, which are made at home daily (or several times a week) on outdoor wood stoves. In the past, animals were not only raised at the ranches; the village was physically smaller, and most households kept a milk cow, chickens, and pigs. This situation is rare today. Nor is much done in the way of vegetable gardening at the houses in the village, and, similar to the pattern that Owen (1959) reported, most of what is grown is sold. However, most houses do have fruit trees, which represents a positive change from the past. When running water was put in all of the houses in the village with a fixed rate for usage, people planted more fruit trees. The fruit is neither canned nor dried; it is all consumed as it ripens, although in earlier times there was a great deal more preservation of all foods. Another change in the present is the decline in use of hunted and gathered foods. Wild fruits, cactus (*nopales*), and wild greens were previously used. While there is still some hunting of deer, quail, and jack rabbits (the latter are often used to feed the dogs), in the past wild pigs were also hunted. Therefore, for both the landless and those with land, Arroyo

Lindo is a wage economy where meat and cheese can be difficult to obtain, milk is bought in cans, and vegetables and some fruits are brought from Hermosillo.

ECONOMIC STRATEGIES IN ARROYO LINDO

Those in the village who have neither cattle nor land either work as laborers for others, have small businesses (*tienda* owners, shoemakers, tire repairers, saddle makers), buy cheese and cattle to sell in Hermosillo, or a few (9) work at a small local mill. Recently a large mine and mill opened close to Arroyo Lindo. Most of the labor force are engineers and other specialized workers who were brought in from further south. However, even some less skilled labor had to be recruited from central Mexico. This fact is surprising in view of the fact that lack of work is cited as a problem of the Sierra, and was given as a reason why many people from Arroyo Lindo have left the village. Reasons given for not wanting to work at the mine include low pay, a dislike of the food served and of one of the bosses, and mothers not wanting their sons to be in contact with those from the south ("*guachos,*" who are simultaneously looked down upon and feared).

The claim of low pay is confusing in that the mine was paying at least the minimum wage. Thus, one real reason may be a preference for having more independence, and more control over one's labor, related to the Sonoran spirit of independence. Another advantage of maintaining more control over one's labor is that of maintaining control over the price of one's labor. In an economy in which inflation in 1982 was at least 100%, and where official increases in the minimum wages are granted by an often slow government bureaucracy, not working for the mine may actually represent the more economically rational decision.

Those who can acquire cattle are also disinclined to work at this type of wage labor. First, in the local culture, ranching is viewed as the ideal lifestyle. Second, ranching can be extremely lucrative, especially for someone with few skills and little formal education. In the spring of 1982, the rancher received 80 pesos per kilo of cheese. About 12 cows must be milked (on the average) to produce 4.5 kilos of cheese. Thus, a rancher with a dozen cows could earn 360 pesos per day (above the rural minimum wage at this time which was slightly less than 300 pesos a day). This advantage for the rancher over the wage earner has maintained itself. In January 1983 the rural minimum wage was 365 pesos a day, while the price of cheese was 140 pesos per kilo, resulting in a daily earning for such a rancher of 630 pesos per day.

ARROYO LINDO LAND PROBLEMS

A primary inescapable problem with the existing economic system is that cows must eat, and so must have access to grazing land or to land that can be planted with cattle fodder. In this area, it is calculated that each cow needs 23.43 hectares of grazing land. According to the 1981 cattle census (Sub' Secretaría de Ganadería 1981) each head in Arroyo Lindo has 7.07 acres. The percentage of overgrazing is therefore calculated to be 231.26% (COTECOCA – Comisíon Técnico Consultiva Para La Determinacíon Regional De Los Coeficientes De Agostadero). Thus a rancher with less than 23.43 hectares per head needs either water to make grass grow or cash with which to buy fodder (which is a less than economically sound approach to dairy farming). It is this need for pasture land or land on which pasture can be grown (and the water to make it grow) that generates many of the more serious problems in the village. The lack of land (which is really a lack of pasture, and ultimately of water) and problems over land tenure are the key problems in Arroyo Lindo that serve to generate intra-village disputes, lack of outside technical assistance, large scale out-migration, and ultimately, nutritional problems. This situation is described below in considerable detail to make clear these linkages. Given that the Sonoran model of development has been held up as a success story (Silvers and Crossen 1980), it seems necessary to make clear not only the village level impact of this type of development policy, but also the subtle and often less than obvious ways in which this impact occurs.

TYPES OF ARROYO LINDO LAND HOLDINGS

Mexican law recognizes three types of landholdings. Small private owners (*pequeños propretarios*) can buy and sell their lands freely. In this region, the legal limit to the lands that one individual can own is about 5,000 hectares. However, in many cases, families have been able to retain ownership of larger tracks by registering portions of the lands in the names of different members of the family. Many such families are among the urban elites of Sonora and thus have high level connections. The ranches of these families are largely used for the production of beef cattle for the export market. *Ejido* lands were granted beginning after the Mexican Revolution, are communally owned and must be more or less continually worked to retain one's rights. In contrast, *comunidad* lands are based on land grants made during the Spanish colonial period and are the property of members of the *comunidad*. These lands need not be worked in order to retain one's rights, and these rights are passed from one generation to the next.

Within the *municipio* (county) of Arroyo Lindo, there are the following landholdings: private lands, owned in the greater part by absentee owners who live in Hermosillo; the *Ejido* Arroyo Lindo, the *Ejido* Sol, and the *comunidad* of Arroyo Lindo (Figure 3). The members of the latter three landholding groups are the residents of the village of Arroyo Lindo and some of their relatives who have migrated to Hermosillo.

Shortly after the Mexican Revolution of 1911, this region of Sonora was characterized by scattered small villages largely surrounded by large land holdings – *latifundios* – used for cattle raising. Since that period, two major changes have taken place. First, beef cattle raising (much of which is for export to the United States) has become an extremely profitable business making the owners of the *latifundios* even more wealthy and powerful. Second, through the granting of *ejidos* and entensions of *ejidos* during the twentieth century, many villages have been able to make some inroads into the lands of the *latifundistas* (large land owners). However, in

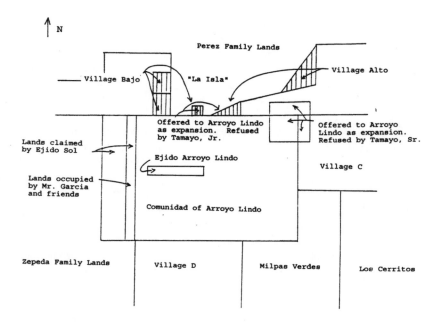

Formerly property of the Perez Family

Figure 3. Schematic Map of the Arroyo Lindo Region. (Not to Scale)

Arroyo Lindo this has not been the case, as it is nearly impossible to organize the whole village on any issue whatsoever. The population is divided into two factions, basically over the issue of land. The key point surrounds the issue of who does and who does not have rights to *communidad* land.

THE *COMUNIDAD*

During the period between the requesting of the title to the *comunidad* lands (19,411 hectares) in 1957, and its granting in 1970, many of the original members of the *comunidad* (210 in all) died (though they have unofficially passed their rights to their sons or widows). Others who feel, for justified reasons, in many cases, that they have rights to these lands, see their main problem to be their neighbors who will not let them enter into what they perceive to be vacant spaces in the *communidad*.

The *comuneros*, on the other hand, claim that the real problem is not within the village. They feel that the basic problem is not enough land to go around and look particularly at the lands of the Perez family, absentee owners, who it is claimed own huge tracts of land – more than what is legal. The Perez family apparently acquired these lands in the late 18th or early 19th century. One estimate of their local landholdings (made by people in Arroyo Lindo) is 67,509 hectares. This figure does not include their holdings on la Costa de Hermosillo and in other parts of northern Mexico. However, the Perez family asserts that the days of unified family holdings are over. The lands were passed intact from the grandfather to his son. This was made possible by government concessions which exempted grazing land from limits placed on size of landholdings an individual could possess (Decreto Concesíon de Inafectabilidad Ganadero, August 14, 1941). This concession expired in 1965. In 1966, according to documents in the Agrarian Reform Archives, the lands were divided among the grandchildren, each of whom is now a *"pequeño proprietario"* – a small landholder – holding below the legal limit of 5,000 hectares. Each ranch is run separately. One of the grandsons whom I interviewed presented himself as a simple man, who was being kept from working and producing. He is afraid to make improvements on his lands, as doing so will raise their cattle carrying capacity. Thus the legal number of hectares he can own will be reduced and he will be subject to expropriation by land hungry villagers whom he views with almost stereotypical contempt.

A certain amount of suspicion on his part is justified, as in recent years he and his cousins (many of whom have intermarried with other powerful upper-class Hermosillo families) have had five land-seeking groups from three different villages soliciting pieces of their lands. The land groups from villages Alto and Bajo have been extremely successful in expanding their *ejidos*. Each of these villages has received three expansions, some of which include lands of the Perez family (although some of the lands village Bajo received are claimed to have been theirs originally, but were stolen by the Perez family). The land groups from Arroyo Lindo, which is a much larger village than villages Alto and Bajo, have on the other hand, met with little success. Much of the problem is due to their lack of ability to reach internal consensus and the fact that the different groups often get in each others' way.

THE NEW POPULATION CENTER

In 1962, 48 people from Arroyo Lindo who are neither members of the comunidad, nor claim that they should be, formed a group to petition for the granting of a new population center within the now divided properties of the Perez family. These men are all landless and work at whatever they can find to do. The group requested these lands of the Perez family as the group maintains that the divisions are illegal; the petition for a new population center was filed before the lands were divided. The earlier petition has priority, and therefore Agrarian Reform cannot continue to consider the ranches of the Perez grandchildren as unavailable for expropriation. As late as 1977, Sonoran Agrarian Reform took the official position, but two officials of that department with whom I spoke in 1982 did agree that the law was on the side of the villagers. However, to date, there has been no progress on this petition, and on several occasions the process has been held up because of requests for land in nearby areas by the other groups in Arroyo Lindo.

THE *EJIDO* SOL

The third land group is that of the *Ejido* Sol (2,460 hectares). This *ejido* was formed in 1966 from territory that had been national land and has 27 members, 20 of whom are still alive. The problem of this *ejido* is largely with family Zepeda, another large absentee landholder. The *ejido* maintains that its land stretches from the west border of the *comunidad*, which is what the maps of the projected boundaries of the *ejido* indicate. However, the definitive map of the *ejido* begins further to the west, the land east of the *ejido* and west of the *comunidad* being occupied by five local private landholders, one of whom (Mr. Garcia) is dominant. He is a distant relative of another wealthy Hermosillo family, and the members of the *Ejido* Sol feel that it is through these family connections that he knows the Zepeda family (this is despite the fact that Garcia is the black sheep of his family).

Without the lands being occupied by the five private owners (590 hectares), the *ejiditarios* claim that the *ejido* does not contain the number of hectares that the title says it should. An official of the *ejido* made two trips to Mexico City – over 1,000 miles distant – financed by contributions by the members of the *ejido*, and found the maps in Mexico City in agreement with the plan that they have. They feel, therefore, that the problem is at the state level. They claim that Agrarian Reform officials are favoring the group of Mr. Garcia. As evidence they cite a recent letter in which Agrarian Reform recognizes as *ejido* officials individuals who are not even members of the *ejido* – but who are associated with Garcia and his group. Mr. Garcia is seen as operating on behalf of the Zepeda family. This is plausible, as it in the Zepeda family's interest, because were the *ejido* not completely occupied with trying to obtain domain over the lands to which it believes it legally has title, it long ago would have sought an expansion into the lands of the Zepeda family. At the present things have quieted down on this front, but a few years back there was violence on both sides, and *ejido* members were repeatedly jailed.

THE *EJIDO* ARROYO LINDO

The last land group in Arroyo Lindo is the *Ejido* Arroyo Lindo (1,236 hectares), consisting of 30 members. This *ejido*, completely within the lands of the *comunidad*, was formed in 1924 as a way of expropriating the lands of a relatively large landowner. Dominated for the past 30 years by the Tamayo family of Arroyo Lindo, the presidency is now in the hands of the other faction within the *ejido*. This faction is made up of *ejido* members who have no cattle. Since they also lack irrigated lands (as does almost everyone in Arroyo Lindo), they plant the lands that they do have, hope for sufficient rain, and for the rest of the time, work at whatever they can find to do in the village.

Recently this faction (19 out of 30 members of the *ejido*) has been trying to organize the *ejido* to request government aid and credit to start some sort of job producing business, such as a chicken or pig raising farm. However, the other faction of the *ejido* has blocked them. A member of the opposing faction explained his opposition was due to the fact that the business would be communal, so they would all just become workers. "And the bad workers, the lazy, would pull the good ones down." He said that he and his companions just wanted to be left in peace to work and produce, but that the others would not let them (this is a common theme among the "haves," including the Perez grandson. The "have nots" say that they also just want to be given a chance to work). The "poultry faction" claims that the real reason the others are opposed to their scheme is that they all have enough cattle to live well. Further, that faction is said to be associated with the Perez family, and are accused of constantly acting to disorganize and paralyze the *ejido*.

The evidence of this collusion with the Perez family that is cited by some members of the *ejido* concerns lands that were twice offered as expansions to the *ejido*, and rejected by members of the Tamayo family, who were then presidents of the *ejido*. In the first case, parts of the lands were those claimed by the *comunidad*. The *ejido* again petitioned for an expansion, and during the presidency of Tamayo, Jr., was offered 1,499 hectares. These were also rejected on the basis of where they were located.

This rejection is almost incomprehensible. No other group had a prior claim to the land, and Agrarian Reform, which had given some of this land provisionally to village Alto in 1972, agreed that Arroyo Lindo had a much better claim to the lands as they were located 9.5 kilometers from village Alto (7 kilometers is the legal limit). Nevertheless, the lands were deemed unacceptable by Tamayo, Jr., the *ejido* president. The lands were then eagerly accepted by villages Alto and Bajo, in spite of the fact that the piece that village Bajo received is not even contiguous to that village's other land holdings. This piece of land, 199 hectares in size, is now referred to by them as "La Isla" (The Island) as it is completely cut off from their other lands by those of the Perez family and the *comunidad* of Arroyo Lindo.

The "poultry faction" of the *ejido* offers an explanation for these unusual events, maintaining that the Tamayo family has close ties with the Perez family; it was the Señor Perez (the grandfather) who donated the fencing to originally fence off the *ejido*. Many of the events regarding the formation and lack of expansion of the *ejido* are clearly in the interest of the Perez family. The location of the *ejido* within the comunidad generates a source of potential intra-village conflict. The awarding of the two pieces of land rejected by the *ejido* to villages Alto and Bajo creates a situation where Arroyo Lindo is now almost completely surrounded by other *ejidos*, and cut off from the possibility of ever acquiring more land (unless, of course, the new population center group is successful). As such, the Perez family will now only be primarily confronted by two villages seeking its lands. However, both of these villages have received three of the four expansions to which they are legally entitled. They thus represent a far lesser threat than does the more populous Arroyo Lindo whose *ejidos* have not received a single expansion. The general belief that the Perez family was trying to "close in" Arroyo Lindo is shared by members of the *comunidad* as well as by people in village Bajo. In 1978, the *ejido*, now under the leadership of the "poultry faction," once again asked for an expansion. This time they were told that there were no available lands within the legal radius (7 kilometers). And in this case, it would seem that Agrarian Reform could hardly be accused of not having tried in the past to comply with the requests of the *ejido*.

THE VILLAGE FEUD

The factions involved in the disputes within the land groups line themselves up in the larger village dispute between those who are in and out of the *comunidad*. This village level dispute should more properly be called a feud, as one's allegiance is largely, though not entirely, determined by kinship ties. However, one may have conflicting ties and side with whichever group presents the best offer at that particular time. While factions often shift, to a large extent the *comunidad*, the "poultry faction" of the *ejido* of Arroyo Lindo, and the five small private landholders involved in the *Ejido* Sol dispute seem to be on one side. The other side includes members of the New Population Center, the *Ejido* Sol, the opposition faction of the *Ejido* Arroyo Lindo, and the local commercial interests (shopkeepers, traders, teachers) most of whom have no land, but many of whom nevertheless do quite well by village standards. Despite their landless state, they may, in some cases, have cattle, and graze them on *comunidad* lands, which infuriates the *comunidad*. The cattle owners claim, however, that they have rights to use land too – and point out that about half of the members of the *comunidad* don't even have cattle.

Actually, at this point in time, it is extremely difficult to tell whose cattle are on whose lands as there are no longer any fences. About four years ago, the feuding parties tore down each other's fences. There has also been destruction of fields. The opposing factions fight over political control of the village. It is impossible to please both factions at the same time. One municipal president of the anti-*comunidad* group, upon beginning to make overtures to the *comunidad* faction, found support from his own group evaporated. About the only thing on which it is possible to obtain complete agreement within the village is the number of people who should be members of the *comunidad*, and the exact number – 210 – is known and cited by all.

The *comunidad* strongly asserts that the Perez family manipulates village politics through its support of the other faction. While collusion with the Perez family is not claimed on the part of all the individuals in the group, it is felt that the leadership in particular is involved. This, like most of the other claims, is plausible, but impossible to prove one way or another. Several individuals associated with the anti-*comunidad* group have had associations with the Perez family, but what these really mean is unclear. On the other hand, it is true that were the village ever able to unite, it might be able to seriously threaten the lands and power of the Perez family.

However, even solutions that do not involve land seem unreachable. The poultry enterprise has been blocked so far. Various groups have approached government agencies for other kinds of development assistance such as wells, irrigation, and credit, but they have been told that nothing can or will be done until the villagers stop fighting among themselves. Therefore, the view in Agrarian Reform is that if the people of Arroyo Lindo have problems, it is their own fault. This attitude is perceived by many as being an excuse being used to favor the interests of the Perez family, in that if Arroyo Lindo prospers at all, it will grow and go after the lands of that family.

Most energy within the village continues to be channeled into the feud, partly due to tradition, but partly due to the economic situation in which people find themselves. Given the relationship of the price of cheese to the minimum wage, those lacking other skills, find it best to try to make a living off the land if at all possible. As a result, they must continue to struggle with their neighbors over land.

LAND PROBLEMS AND SELECTIVE OUT-MIGRATION

Given all of the above, it would seem that the problem would not be to explain why anyone would leave Arroyo Lindo, but rather why anyone would stay. Life in Arroyo Lindo at this point is a zero-sum game – one neighbor's gain is another's loss. There are few, if any, opportunities to get ahead. Those who are better off are largely on the defensive against their landless and/or cowless neighbors. A positively selective pattern of out-migration, where those with the most education and skills are those who leave, thus grows out of the village land situation. A potential migrant has few resources that he/she can convert to capital for use in the city (since neither *communidad* nor *ejido* lands can be sold). Therefore, the risk involved in leaving is very high for many. Further, as discussed above, the nature of the cheese market encourages the less skilled to stay at home.

The operation of these forces is seen by comparing educational levels of those who have remained in Arroyo Lindo to those who have left. Adult migrants of both genders have completed more years of schooling than have their non-migrant relatives. Mean incomes of the Arroyo Lindo sample were lower than those of their urban siblings and cousins, both at the household level (326,952 – non-migrants versus 368,748 – migrants), as well as on a per capita basis (38,210 – non-migrants versus 59,685 – migrants). It should be noted that the higher per capita income of the migrants more than makes up for a higher urban cost of living, assuming

that the 13.7% difference in the rural versus urban minimum wages represents the difference in costs of living; average migrant per capita income is
64% higher than that of non-migrants.

This evidence strongly suggests a pattern of positive selectivity among
the migrants that operates not only among families, but within them as
well. The land problems make it difficult to achieve a better standard of living in Arroyo Lindo (migrants list "no work" as one reason they have left –
a push factor). The land problems also mean that one's children are likely
to be in the same situation. Thus the pull factor (the lure into the city) most
often mentioned by the migrants – more schooling opportunities for their
children – must be viewed as not simply an independent characteristic of
the city, but as related to the conditions imposed by the land problems and
other push factors (which create the impetus to leave the rural areas).

To an extent, out-migration relieves pressure on the land by reducing
the number of people who need the land. However, it also exacerbates the
problem, in that leaving does not automatically require one to relinquish
one's right to land. In fact, the migrant has everything to gain and nothing
to lose by holding on to his or her land – nothing to lose, that is, but the
good will of one's former neighbors who deeply resent the city dwellers
who have other means of making a livelihood yet continue to use scarce
rangeland.

Regardless of which village faction one chooses to believe, there is little
doubt that from an objective point of view the population segment that
benefits from the conditions that have been created in the countryside is
the one represented by the Perez family. Given the unexpandable land (and
therefore pasture) base and lack of access to sources of assistance to produce more grass (i.e., irrigation, wells, and pumps), ranchers in Arroyo
Lindo must spend large amounts of money on food for their animals. As
their cash needs increase, they try to generate income in other ways –
which may in part account for the large number of *tiendas* and other small
businesses that are largely operated by the women. Many of the families
with larger numbers of cattle seem to employ this strategy. However, if the
manner of intensification is to increase the number of cattle on the range,
people and cattle begin to compete for the same food money. By selling
steers, a typical rancher in Arroyo Lindo will earn annually only about one
half of what it costs to buy food for the animals. Thus, about one fifth to
one sixth of the earnings from the sale of cheese must be used to buy fodder. (Note, however, that this distribution still results in a daily wage that
is above the minimum [80% of 630 = 504 pesos/day – Jan. 1983]). Yet the
cattle must eat, or they will produce nothing at all. Fortunately, the increases
in cheese prices have enabled people to at least hold their ground against
inflation.

Furthermore, the villagers are increasingly forced into the least prof-itable end of the cattle business. If one is buying food for cattle, then those cattle that are not producing income must be sold. Thus, there is tremen-dous pressure to sell the steers when they are young. Their sale also gener-ates income to be used to buy food for the cows that can be milked. These steers are either bought by the larger private ranchers (such as the Perez Family) or eventually by feedlots in Hermosillo. The villagers thus assume a great part of the cost and risk of raising the beef cattle (as this cost and risk occurs in the first few months of the animals' lives) yet receive only a small percentage of the ultimate profit. This situation parallels the migra-tion pattern in which human resources are raised, yet the village does not derive much profit from this "business" either.

The migration to Hermosillo and other Sonoran cities continues the cycle as it increases the demand for cheese in those areas. But the selective nature of the out-migration creates a situation in which those who are left have the least chance of being able to solve the problems which encour-aged their relatives to leave in the first place. Some of the same skills that the Arroyo Lindo migrants possess and that enable them to do as well as they do in the city are exactly the kinds of skills that the village needs to solve its problems. These traits include initiative, more advanced educa-tion, sophistication, and the ability to deal with the urban elite. Those who remain are those who are in the least favorable position to take risks and who have to hold on to the little that they have. Their best chances lie in continuing to struggle for land, while trying to ensure that their children have access to as much training and education as possible – so that they can also "afford" to leave.

ARROYO LINDO: SUMMARY

The ethnographic data suggest several social factors that may be related to the nutritional problems observed in Arroyo Lindo. The shift to a market economy over the past few decades may have been important. In the pre-sent, there seem to be linkages among the type of development that has taken place in Sonora as a whole, the land problems, positively selective out-migration, and the presence of nutritional problems. Arroyo Lindo's malnutrition may be in large measure income-related. For those who remain in Arroyo Lindo, two potential social sources of nutritional prob-lems can be identified: the difficulty of making a living for those without cattle, and the difficulty of making a living for those with cattle.

HERMOSILLO

Hermosillo has grown tremendously in recent years (1980 population –
281,697 inhabitants [Estado de Sonora 1980]), largely due to rural to
urban migration within Sonora, as well as some migration from areas of
Mexico further to the south. This rapid growth indicates why it was relatively difficult to locate a sample of households in which both husband
and wife were born in the city. The capital of the state, Hermosillo exhibits
distinctly Sonoran characteristics, which I saw in my first days in the city:

> "A frantic few days of arriving and settling in – made much more compli-
> cated by the complete lack of almost any place to stay in the entire city. This
> is due to the presence in town of a baseball championship, whose players
> and fans have filled all hotels and most other places as well. Baseball, or
> "beisbol," for days now the local madness, seems to affect other aspects of
> life as well, as almost everything, including many university classes, grinds
> to a halt when one of the games is on the T.V. Poor Geertz, if he were here,
> he'd have to study baseball instead of cockfights." (Field notes, Feb. 1982).

> "It was in the paper today that some American soldiers had landed their
> helicopter by mistake just over the Mexican border. When this was being
> talked about at lunch, I made the comment that they'd better watch out, as
> the last time U.S. soldiers came to Mexico, they took California, Texas,
> Arizona, and New Mexico. Laura's comment was, 'that's ok, they can take
> Sonora – I'll go.'" (Field notes, June 1982).

Many of Erasmus' (1961) observations made in towns in southern
Sonora apply to Hermosillo in the present. There is a large middle class,
and there appears to be considerable social mobility (Ruiz: personal communication). Consumer goods of all types are in large demand, and are
purchased, if at all possible, in the United States because some items are in
limited supply due to the distance of Hermosillo from the centers of production further south. Moreover, until recently, business was controlled by
a few powerful intermarried families, a situation that limited competition
and availability of many types of consumer goods. Finally, there is the
prestige associated with anything purchased in the United States.

Twenty years ago, Hermosillo was a dusty town with only two or three
paved streets but it has rapidly grown into a lovely city of broad tree-lined
boulevards. City services, such as paved roads and running water, have not
been able to keep pace with the rapid population growth (particularly in
the areas on the northern and southern edges of the city), but Hermosillo
is largely a city that works. Potholes are fixed, parks are maintained.
Hermosillo's cleanliness and air of being well kept up is particularly
marked when contrasted with Guaymas. An hour to the south, the port city
of Guaymas seems dirty and run down by comparison. Hermosillo is not

an industrial city; major employers include food processing companies, and a cement plant, located southeast of the city. Hermosillo also serves as a service and shopping center for the villages of the Sierra to the east, and for the large-scale irrigation areas to the west – *la costa*.

THE MIGRANTS

As discussed previously, the characteristics of the migrants in the sample show a clear pattern of positive selectivity over their rural siblings. Even in casual conversations with the migrants, frequent topics of discussion included descriptions of their efforts to better themselves, their lives, and their children's futures. Many of the migrants, particularly the women, showed levels of initiative far surpassing those of their rural relatives, even those in similar economic straits. For example, Carmen works as a maid all week and then on the weekends has a taco stand. Investments in children's educations are a high priority; Raul and Marta live with their ten children in a two room house, but have managed to educate the children to a point where their daughter is a teacher, their son an electrician, and another son is finishing high school (*prepa*). The migrants live throughout the city, although many cluster in the lower middle class neighborhoods of Paloverde and Piedra Bola in the southern part of Hermosillo. Only four of the households lived in neighborhoods considered to be economically marginal, and by income and living standards, only two could be classified as such. The Arroyo Lindo migrants have no formal associations, nor do they represent an interaction community. Relationships between migrants are based on Arroyo Lindo kinship ties, as opposed to migrant status. Ties to Arroyo Lindo are strong, and trips to visit relatives there are common. In addition, some migrant households have economic ties to Arroyo Lindo, including those who have ranches and cattle there, as well as those who buy cheese in Arroyo Lindo to sell in Hermosillo. Migrant husbands had lived in Hermosillo for 2–23 years (mean 10.6 years); wives had lived there for 2–22 years (mean 10.3 years).

THOSE BORN IN THE CITY

The sample of those born in the city covered the total range of incomes. The higher end of the continuum was represented by Dora's household. Her husband is a member of one of the large absentee landowning families involved in the Arroyo Lindo disputes. She has two maids, cupboards and refrigerator full of United States products such as brown sugar, parmesan cheese, mustard, mayonnaise, and vinegar, and was always very busily occupied with charity affairs. Another household of similar economic circumstances had a carpeted living room with wicker furniture, and Chinese wall hangings that had been bought on visits to Disneyland and Sea World.

The lower end of the continuum was represented by Lupita's household. For 11 years, they have lived in a shack in the neighborhood of Valdo del Rio, which was the riverbed before the river was dammed up. The neighborhood's low location causes it to be flooded in periods of rain. Their house has one room, which has no electricity, an adobe wood stove, two beds, a table and very little other furniture. This neighborhood is unusual in several respects. The women are very isolated; they get out of their houses very little – not even to weddings, baptisms, etc. Many of them did not even have weddings of their own. Many of the households in this neighborhood are headed by women who have been deserted by their husbands. Another unusual finding among these, the poorest of those born in the city, was that several toddlers over 1 and 1/2 years old were still being breast-fed. In all other sample populations, babies are breast-fed for a maximum of three months. The persistence of breast feeding in Valdo del Rio may be related to the economic situation of these households, and would lead to the conclusion that extended breast feeding is of very low prestige. This situation should be kept in mind by nutritionists seeking to decrease bottle feeding of babies in this region.

THE AMERICANS

"Then I went over to see Julia, an American who is married to a Mexican. When I got there, they had just finished eating breakfast. On the table was Lady Lee brand peanut butter and Log Cabin syrup. The kitchen included a dishwasher, microwave, and food processor – all of which are rare among Mexican households of similar income levels" (Field notes, Dec. 1982).

The community of Americans living permanently in Hermosillo consists of around 200 individuals (this includes children of households with at least one American parent). While there are some families in which both spouses are from the United States, the most common situation is that of an American woman married to a Mexican man. In the households sampled, the American wives had lived in Hermosillo from 2–35 years (mean 10 years). Though there is not an intense sense of group identification as Americans, the group can be considered a community in terms of interaction among its members. All of the households are extremely well off economically.

The total American population is considered by its members to consist of three subgroups, which are important to them in terms of social interactions. The divisions seem to be based on similarity of views and values among the American wives, and represent general groupings, rather than neat pigeonholes that would have value for analytic purposes. Ethnic background of the wife does not seem to be related to grouping; the Mexican-American women do not cluster in any one of the groups.

The first group is an older, richer, more aristocratic set, very few of whom were part of the sample due to their ages and/or lack of children still residing at home. The next subgroup is called by some of its members "the dissidents," which refers to how they perceive their relationship with the first subgroup. Most of the "dissident" women are married to Mexicans who are either intellectuals, or medical or other professionals. Almost all of these women maintain some level of contact with other American women, particularly those who share their liberal social values. Many of them met their husbands while the latter were studying in the United States, and admit to not really having had any idea what they were getting themselves into. Living in a foreign country is a relatively intense form of culture contact; being married to someone from another culture adds further to the intensity. It is not surprising therefore, that these women feel intensely the conflicts and contradictions of life between cultures.

The third group is comprised of two subgroups, labelled the "Christians" and the missionaries, among whom there is less interaction than among the dissidents. The missionaries are active professionals, while the Christians are more of a social group. Nevertheless, there are a great number of shared values among the Christian and missionary wives. For example, both Christian and missionary women tend to be in favor of school prayer and are advocates of the teaching of creationism.

Another difference between the missionaries and Christians is in terms of nationality of their husbands. The missionaries are married to other Americans. But background of the husband is not the criterion for inclusion in this group, as is seen in the categorization as a "dissident" of one woman who is married to an American, and both of whom are involved in Quaker activities. The missionaries, on the whole, tend to have a very positive outlook. For Liz, Hermosillo "was home," and she really liked living there.

The Christians are American women who had married Mexicans and moved to that country. They meet for Bible classes weekly. The outlook of many of this group also tends to be more optimistic than that of many of the dissidents. When asked how she felt about living in Mexico, Joan said, "I see my order of duty as God, my husband, and my family, so that the country where I live is of lesser importance." However, some of this attitude may be due to the influence that religion has had on the lives of these women. A number of the Christians told me that they had become more interested in religion since coming to Hermosillo. Susan said, "I was very isolated until I found the American Bible study group. It has really helped me cope." Betty felt, "I couldn't have managed living in Mexico without my faith."

Both the Christians and the dissidents have definite opinions as to what they like and dislike about life in Hermosillo. They focus on the points where the two cultures differ most. All of the American women disliked the conservatism and materialism of Hermosillo, which they see as a closed, insular society. Some mentioned that they found people unfriendly, and also found few people with whom they had much in common, resulting in much loneliness. Other complaints included the quality of education and medical care, bad and slow service in stores, the importance of class differences and the way people treated those in classes lower than their own.

The American women also disliked the separation in Mexican culture of men's and women's lives. During the period of courtship a couple is constantly together. Once married, however, the men often prefer to socialize with their male friends. Yet, the American women say, Mexican women won't go out, to the movies for example, without their husbands.

Even the Mexican Americans who had married Mexicans reported problems of adjustment and unfriendliness. Andrea found it hard to deal with people in Hermosillo, and felt that "Mexicans are unwilling to wait their turns." She also objected to the fact that "you need influence to get things done." Another Mexican American woman, Beth, felt that children in Mexico had too little responsibility and too much liberty. She also found "Mexicans are less open, more concerned with doing the right things, and very much more concerned with formality in dress than are Americans."

In spite of not liking certain aspects of Mexican society, the American women do recognize numerous positive aspects of life in Mexico, such as less crime and a less hurried lifestyle. Nancy said, "the Mexican environment is much better for my children; there's less peer pressure, and fewer drugs in the schools." Linda noted, "I'd have to work if I lived in the United States." She added, "the American women who complain about living in Hermosillo only think they'd be happier at home. But they really wouldn't be."

In summary, the observations of the American women about life in Mexico focused on the points at which the two cultures are least similar. These include formality/informality, extent of class differences, and patterns of interaction between men and women. The extent to which they feel the impact of these cultural differences largely results in negative feelings about their lives in Mexico and eventually hampers their ability to feel culturally comfortable in their living situations. The Americans married to Americans tend to have lived in Hermosillo for longer periods of time (and tend to be the most positive), while the Mexican-Americans married to Mexicans tend to be more recent arrivals (and tend to be the most negative); nevertheless, my association with these women leads me to believe that it is not the length of residence that is the key factor. The Americans married to Americans were much more shielded from Mexico – within their homes there could be as much or as little of Mexico and Mexican culture as they chose to admit. The Mexican-Americans were probably under the most pressure to fit in – after all, they were at least part Mexican, if only by background, and within their homes, Mexico, in the form of their husbands, was constantly present.

COOKING AND DIETARY PATTERNS IN SONORA

The distinct style characteristic of Sonora also applies to the types of foods used. In contrast to stereotypes common in the United States and patterns seen in Central Mexico, Sonoran food uses very little chile; the dominant spice is coriander (cilantro). The elaborate chile based sauces common in Central Mexico, incorporating a variety of ingredients, are not used in Sonora. For example, on the rare occasion when *mole* is made, canned *mole* sauce is used. The preferred tortilla is flour, not corn (although consumption of corn tortillas was more common about 30 years ago). Vegetable use is quite limited, with those traditionally used being squash, cabbage, garlic, green chile, green beans, and onions; use of meat, especially beef is very common. *Queso regional*, which is similar to cottage cheese is used extensively. Also commonly used are limes, which are squeezed into soups and on vegetables, fruits, and even Chinese food.

However, the types of dishes and the order in which they are served are similar to those of Mexico as a whole. For the mid-day meal, the first course is a *sopa* which can be wet or dry. Wet *sopa* is any soup with any form of rice or pasta in it; dry *sopas* (which are more common) use these starches, but they are cooked with tomato and bouillon until the liquid is absorbed. In all *sopas*, the starch is always first fried, or browned in oil. The only *sopa* I encountered that does not contain rice or pasta is squash (similar to zucchini) and cheese; perhaps it is included in this category because the zucchini is first fried. A *sopa* can be used alone, and often is in poorer households. In wealthier households, it is followed by another dish, usually containing meat. If the meat (which usually is first boiled) is later fried with other ingredients, the dish is called a *guisado*. An alternate meal pattern is that of the one pot meal, which is often a *caldo* (thick soup). What distinguishes a *caldo* from a wet *sopa* is the lack of rice or pasta in the former.

Kitchen facilities vary by income level. The poorest urban households will use wood for indoor cooking; those in rural areas will use an outdoor wooden stove made out of an old oil barrel. The rest of the kitchen facilities will consist of a wooden table with two to four chairs. Slightly better off households will have a gas stove, as well as a cabinet in which to keep pots, dishes, etc. Kitchen sinks are very rare in rural areas, but less so in the cities. Higher income households have kitchen facilities much like those of middle class Americans.

DIETARY DATA COLLECTION

I used standard qualitative anthropological research techniques of participant observation, which included living with families in the communities being studied, enabling the observation of daily diets and food habits. A variety of quantitative techniques were also used. For each household, an interview on aspects of household economics and food utilization was conducted with the female head of household, as it is she who generally has responsibility in these areas. In addition, food consumption data were collected by quantitative recall for each individual in the household for two weekdays as well as for Sunday, a day on which food consumption tends to differ from that of the rest of the week. Consumption was recorded as to whether it was consumed at home or away from home. "Eating out" was defined as all food from non-household sources consumed outside of the household, regardless of whether other household members were present, and regardless of whether the food was purchased or not.

Mean daily individual consumption of ten food types was calculated as standardized servings, adapted from the Michigan Department of Public Health exchange system (see Table 5). It was decided to focus on foods rather than on nutrients, as the later approach often obscures shifts in diet that may be important in terms of impact on the household budget, although the nutritional impact of such changes may be minimal at the individual level. For example, a shift from egg to meat consumption has minimal effects on protein consumption, but is a much more expensive source of similar nutrients. The ten food types chosen were based on the basic food groups, expanded to cover the range of culturally important food categories in this area. The food types are as follows:

Fruit (FRUIT) – oranges, watermelon, bananas, limes, quince.

Vegetables (VEG) – zucchini, lettuce, cabbage, onions, carrots, tomatoes, green chile, red chile, peas, chile sauce, spinach and other greens, fresh coriander, cucumber.

Beans (BEANS) – pinto beans, garbanzo beans, lentils.

Dairy (DAIRY) – fresh milk, evaporated milk, powdered milk, regional cheese (similar to cottage cheese), canned cream, Chihuahua cheese (similar to monterey jack), asadero cheese (similar to mozzarella), ice cream, yogurt.

Eggs (EGGS) – chicken eggs.

Grains (GRAINS) – flour tortillas, corn tortillas, bread, all varieties of pasta products, *pan dulce* (sweet rolls), rice, cake, crackers, cold and cooked cereal.

Miscellaneous (MISC) – soda, candy, Kool-Aid, potato chips (and related foods, i.e., Fritos, Doritos, etc.)

Potatoes (POT) – white potatoes.

Meat (MEAT) – beef and pork (both with very little fat trimmed), chicken, tuna, cold cuts, sausage, fish, turtle, very little of variety meats other than *menudo* (tripe) and *cabeza* (beef head).

Alcohol (ALC) – beer, mixed drinks.

Table 5. Mean Food Consumption for Arroyo Lindo, Migrants, Urban Born, and Households with American Wives (in Mean Daily Per Capita Servings)

N	Arroyo Lindo		Migrants		Urban-Born		American Wives
	LI	*HI*	*LI*	*HI*	*LI*	*HI*	
	135	63	88	78	84	71	121
Food Type							
Fruit	0.6	0.6	0.6	1.1	0.4	1.1	1.3
Veg	0.7	0.9	0.8	1.0	0.5	1.2	1.3
Beans	2.2	1.1	2.1	0.8	1.8	0.6	0.4
Dairy	0.8	0.6	1.3	1.6	1.1	1.8	1.9
Eggs	1.1	1.1	0.9	0.8	0.8	0.9	0.8
Grains	7.1	5.4	6.6	5.0	6.0	4.4	5.2
Misc	1.3	1.3	1.7	1.7	1.0	0.8	0.7
Pot	0.5	0.3	0.5	0.4	0.4	0.3	0.3
Meats	0.7	1.5	1.1	2.1	1.2	1.9	1.7
Alc	0.1	0.2	0.1	0.3	0.2	0.1	0.2

LI – Lower Income; HI – Higher Income.
Serving Units: Fruit – 1/2 c juice or cooked/canned or 1 medium piece; Vegetable – 1/2 c juice or cooked/canned or 3/4 c raw; Beans – 1/2 c cooked; Dairy – 1 c milk or 1 c plain yogurt or 1 1/3 oz. aged cheese; Eggs – 1 medium egg; Grains – 1 slice bread or 3/4 c cooked cereal, spaghetti, noodles; Misc – 1 soft drink (473 ml) or 1 small package potato chips, etc. or 1 medium sized candy bar or 1 c Kool-Aid; Potato – 1 medium; Meat – 2 to 3 oz. cooked meat/fish; Alcohol – 1 can beer or 1 mixed drink or 1/2 c wine.

The standard servings were converted into a daily average for each individual by multiplying the standard servings consumed on each of the weekdays by three, adding Sunday's consumption, and dividing the total by seven. Only individuals between one and sixty years were included in the calculation of the group means presented.

ARROYO LINDO DIETARY PATTERNS

Diet, in many ways, follows the pattern noted by Owen (1959) for the village he studied. Households of lower incomes consume greater amounts of dairy, beans, potatoes, and grains and lesser amounts of vegetables and meat than do households of higher incomes (Table 5). Few differences are seen in consumption of fruit, eggs, miscellaneous (MISC), and alcohol. Other aspects of Arroyo Lindo food consumption patterns are given in Table 6.

HERMOSILLO DIETARY PATTERNS: OVERVIEW

Little food for local consumption is produced in the area around Hermosillo. Most of what is grown on *la costa* is for export, and areas in the central eastern part of the city that were vegetable farms 30 years ago are now the neighborhoods of Los Arcos and Valle Verde. Vegetables now come from Sinaloa, the state to the south. There are three markets in the city, but most major shopping is done at supermarkets or co-operatives for federal or state workers (which are less expensive than the supermarkets). In addition, one is never far from a *tienda*. Typically, tiendas stock canned and other dry kinds of foods, such as pasta, flour, and sugar. Occasionally, a limited amount of fresh fruits and vegetables and cheese may be available.

Eating out is quite popular. There is one Kentucky Fried Chicken, and there are many hamburger places, as well as pizza, Chinese, and other restaurants, but much eating out is done on the street. Open air taco stands abound, and are crowded at appropriate times of the day (evening for *tacos de carne asada* [steak], weekends and mornings for *tacos de cabeza* [head] and *tacos de cahuama* [turtle]). Also available on the streets in the evenings are hot dogs, or in Spanish, "hot dogs," which are served with chopped tomatoes and onions. As in Arroyo Lindo, *tortas* (sub sandwiches) are frequently sold near schools, and are purchased by the students, along with soft drinks, Fritos, fruit, candy, etc. during their recess periods. An alternative to street or fast food (no frozen food is available in Hermosillo) is prepared food from the supermarkets, and food from the numerous "super cocinas," which feature homemade food that is taken home in the purchaser's own pot and reheated. The quality of the food is excellent, although it is somewhat expensive.

HERMOSILLO DIETARY PATTERNS: THE MIGRANTS

Mean food consumption for each of the ten food types for the migrant sample (at higher and lower incomes) is presented in Table 5. The lower income households consume greater amounts of beans and grains, and lesser amounts of fruit, vegetables, dairy, meat, and alcohol than do the higher income households. Little or no difference is seen in consumption of MISC, eggs, and potatoes. Other aspects of the migrants' food consumption patterns are given in Table 6.

For lower income households, changes in food consumption associated with the move to Hermosillo included increased fruit consumption. Increased milk and cheese consumption was reported by some, although some who had had ranches in Arroyo Lindo reported the opposite pattern.

All of the migrant households noted a decrease in home production of food in their lifetimes. Among those of higher incomes, 27% associated these changes with their move to the city. Forty-five percent of higher income households reported no changes due to their urban residence (but half of these said the lack of change was a result of having bought food in Hermosillo even when they lived in Arroyo Lindo).

HERMOSILLO DIETARY PATTERNS: THOSE BORN IN THE CITY

Mean food consumption for each of the ten food types for those born in the city (at higher and lower incomes) is presented in Table 5. Other aspects of food consumption are given in Table 6.

HERMOSILLO DIETARY PATTERNS: THE AMERICANS

The American women had definite opinions on the topic of food availability and quality in Mexico. One of the most common complaints was of the limited availability of many foods in Hermosillo. For some, the problem was not Mexico as a whole, but Hermosillo; they stressed a better situation in Mexico City, particularly with respect to variety of vegetables. Another problem encountered in Hermosillo was that of refrigerated milk going bad in a short period of time – often in one day in the summer. Several women also had had problems with canned or packaged foods, in terms of the quality of the former, and bugs in the latter.

Table 6. Dietary Patterns of Sample Groups

Dietary Pattern	Arroyo Lindo		Migrants		Urban Born		Americans
	Lower Income	Higher Income	Lower Income	Higher Income	Lower Income	Higher Income	
Home Production:							
Vegetable Gardens	13%	0%	11%	0%	17%	0%	11%
Fruit Trees	80%	100%	67%	46%	44%	50%	76%
Egg Production	60%	0%	33%	9%	28%	0%	0%
Shopping:							
Village	✓	✓	—	—	—	—	—
Hermosillo:							
Tiendas	✓	—	✓	—	—	—	—
Supermarket	✓	✓	✓	✓	✓	✓	✓
City Market	—	—	✓	✓	✓	—	✓
Speciality Stores (for meat, fruits or vegetables)	—	—	—	—	—	—	—
Co-Operatives	—	—	—	—	—	✓	✓
U.S.:							
When	7% – buying clothing	40% – buying clothing	11% – buying clothing	55% – buying clothing	44% – buying clothing or visiting relatives	85% – buying clothing or seeing a doctor	78% – buying clothing or visiting relatives, or doing business. 22% – regular shopping trips to U.S. items unavailable in Mexico
Why	better quality	items unavailable in Mexico	items unavailable in Mexico	better quality	better quality	better quality and cheaper prices	

Meal Times:							
Breakfast	7:45	7:45	8:15	7:30	7:45	7:15	7:15
Comida	1:45	1:45	2:00	2:20	2:00	2:30	2:30
Cena	7:00	7:45	7:45	7:30	7:15	7:15	7:30
Breakfast Format:							
Eggs/Oatmeal	most	most	most	most	most	most	most
Beans	most	most	most	—	some	—	—
Flour Tortillas	most	most	most	most	some	—	—
Coffee	most	most	most	most	some	—	—
Milk with Coffee	some	most	most	some	—	—	—
Meat	some	most	some	some	—	half	some
Beans and Cheese	—	—	—	most	—	—	—
Bread	—	—	—	some	most	most	most
Milk	—	—	—	some	some	most	most
Fruit/Juice	—	—	—	—	—	some	some
Cold Cereal	—	—	—	—	—	—	a few
Toast	—	—	—	—	—	—	a few
Comida Format:							
Caldo	some	—	a few	some	very few	—	—
Sopa	some	most	some	some	some	most	most
Beans	most	most	most	most	most	most	some
Corn Tortillas	most	most	most	most	most	most	most
Coffee/Soda	most	—	most	—	some	—	—
Main Dish/Meat	some	most	a few	a few	a few	most	most
Vegetables	—	—	—	some	—	some	most
Dessert	—	—	—	—	—	some	most
Bread	—	—	—	—	—	a few	most
"Starch"	—	—	—	—	—	—	a few
Salad	—	—	—	—	—	—	a few

Table 6. (Continued)

Dietary Pattern	Arroyo Lindo		Migrants		Urban Born		Americans
	Lower Income	Higher Income	Lower Income	Higher Income	Lower Income	Higher Income	
Cena Format:							
Beans/Beans with Cheese	most	most	most	most	most	some	—
Fried Potatoes	most	most	most	some	most	—	—
Flour Tortillas	most	most	most	most	most	—	—
Coffee	most	most	some	most	—	—	—
Meat	a few	most	some	—	some	—	—
Sandwiches	—	a few	—	a few	a few	some	some
Leftovers	—	a few	—	a few	a few	some	a few
Milk/Cafe Con Leche	—	—	some	—	some	—	—
Cold Cereal	—	—	—	—	—	some	—
Eggs	—	—	—	—	—	some	some
Licuado (Fruit and Milk)	—	—	—	—	—	some	—
Quesadilla (Cheese and Flour Tortilla)	—	—	—	—	—	some	—
Hot Dogs	—	—	—	—	—	—	some
Canned Soup	—	—	—	—	—	—	some

	1	2	3	4	5	6	7
One Pot Meals:							
Used?	100%	80%	89%	100%	83%	55%	52%
Liked?	100%	80%	89%	100%	83%	70%	50%
Main Starch:							
Flour Tortillas	100%	100%	100%	73%	72%	40%	—
Rice	—	—	—	9%	—	—	—
Pasta	—	—	—	9%	—	—	—
Bread	—	—	—	9%	17%	25%	50%
Potatoes	—	—	—	—	—	15%	25%
Rice	—	—	—	—	—	—	25%
Weekend Meals:							
Saturday Later	20%	20%	22%	9%	39%	60%	67%
Sunday Later	20%	40%	56%	36%	50%	85%	67%
Ways of cooking:							
Meat:							
Boiled then Fried	✓	✓	✓	✓	✓	✓	
Broiled	✓	—	✓	—	—	✓	✓
Fried	✓	✓	✓	✓	✓	✓	✓
Baked/Broiled	—	—	—	—	—	—	✓
Starches:							
Fried then Boiled	✓	✓	✓	✓	✓	✓	✓
Boiled	—	—	—	✓	—	✓	✓

Table 6. (*Continued*)

Dietary Pattern	Arroyo Lindo		Migrants		Urban Born		Americans
	Lower Income	Higher Income	Lower Income	Higher Income	Lower Income	Higher Income	
Vegetables:							
Raw	✓	✓	✓	✓	✓	✓	✓
Boiled	✓	✓	✓	✓	✓	✓	✓
Fried then Boiled	✓	✓	—	—	—	—	—
Steamed	—	—	—	—	—	—	✓
Key Factors in Food Choices:							
Taste	1	1	2	1	2	1	—
Expense	1	—	1	2	1	2	—
Time	—	—	—	3	—	—	1

During 1982, availability of all products was sporadic. Due to the rate of inflation and government controlled prices, producers often created artificial shortages to force price increases. Hermosillo has only a certain range of fresh products available. The Americans complained that they couldn't use their American cookbooks because they couldn't get the necessary ingredients, yet Sonorans trying to use Mexican cookbooks developed for the central part of the country had similar problems.

Some of the problems the Americans encountered with food availability and quality may be due to their culture's style of cooking, as well as their cultural patterns of food purchasing. Sonoran cooking is based on foods traditionally available in the region. Thus, Sonorans, who use a narrower range of fruits, and particularly vegetables, than do Americans, perceive fewer problems of limited variety. Sonorans also tend to purchase items as needed, rather than keeping a stock on hand. Patricia, an upper-middle class Sonoran woman from Hermosillo, told me she didn't have any idea how long refrigerated milk kept, as she always bought it daily.

The comments of the Americans about Mexican food quality were not all negative. It was noted that relative prices of fruits and vegetables were lower in Mexico than in the United States and that there was less processing of food in Mexico which made the food more nutritious.

However, the frequency with which comments about food availability were made – Donna defined American food as "a lot of variety – the availability of anything you feel like eating" – suggests that deeper meanings may be at play here. One of the most basic values for Americans is that of control, and lack of control over many of the events that affect one's life is a fact of life in Mexico. Adjustment to this aspect of Mexican life is one of the hardest parts of living in that country. As such, it is not surprising that the lack of control over even the variety of foods from which to choose in the supermarket – having control taken from them by lack of choice – emerges as the most important aspect of the diets of these American women, as they themselves see it.

One way for the American women to re-establish control, at least over their diets, is to remove themselves from the Mexican food environment. While the Americans did some of their food shopping in Hermosillo supermarkets, all additionally reported buying food in the United States. 22% made regular food shopping trips to Tucson (a 4–5 hour drive on a narrow two lane road). Other food shopping in the U.S. was done in conjunction with trips to buy clothes, visit relatives, or conduct business. A long list of U.S. products is purchased, largely because of their unavailability in Mexico (see Table 7). This shopping list is not only longer than those of any of the previous groups' lists, but it also reveals much about the Americans as a group. While favorite U.S. foods of other groups (such

Table 7. U.S. Shopping Purchases of "Americans"

Fruits and Vegetables	Dairy Products	Meats	Other
Frozen Orange Juice	Cheese	Canned Ravioli	Mayonnaise
Raisins	Macaroni and Cheese Mix	Hot Dogs	Butter
Dried Fruits	Yogurt	"Meat"	Salad Dressing
Sweet Corn	Parmesan Cheese	Chicken	Cake Mixes
Broccoli	Milk	Canned Ham	Whipping Cream
Mushrooms		Spam	Puddings
Pears		Deviled Ham	Spices
Apples		Tuna	Bisquik
Strawberries		Corned Beef	Nuts
Peaches		Leg of Lamb	Peanut Butter
Lettuce		Canned Clams	Margarine
Artichokes		Canned Oysters	Canned Mincemeat
Cherry Tomatoes		Bacon	Dream Whip
Honeydew Melons		Cold Cuts	Sweets
Frozen Vegetables		Roasts	Cakes
Pickles		Smoked Clams	Garlic Vinegar
Canned Pumpkin		Meat Sauces	Malt Vinegar
Canned Cranberries			Chocolate Chips
Canned Sweet Potatoes			Coconut
Canned Fruit Cocktail			Cold Cereal
Pie Fillings			Cookies
Apple Juice			Crackers
Cranberry Juice			Instant Low Calorie Tea
Relishes			Brownie Mix
			Snacking Cake Mix

Boxed Stuffing
Marshmallow Creme
Rice
Rye Bread
Jelly
Cornmeal
Black Tea
Brown Sugar
Dry Soup Mix
Wheat Germ
Tapioca
Sunflower Seeds
Kool Aid
Cocoa
Crisco
Dehydrated Spaghetti
  Sauce Mix
Ice Cream Topping
Seafood Seasoning
Ding Dongs
Zingers
Black Olives
Baking Chocolate
Granola
English Muffins
Granola Bars
Dry Roasted Peanuts
Raisin Bread

as mayonnaise, margarine, and canned seafood) appear, so also do a larger number of "convenience foods" (macaroni and cheese mix, spaghetti sauce mix) and "health foods" (wheat germ, granola). Also included are foods used on U.S. holidays (such as canned pumpkin and cranberries), and types of meat not usually used by Mexicans (leg of lamb, corned beef). In summary, the Americans were less than completely satisfied with the foods they could purchase in Mexico, and dealt with the problem – took control of it – by shopping in the U.S. as much as possible.

Mean food consumption for each of the ten food types for the sample of households with American wives is presented in Table 5. Other aspects of this group's food consumption patterns are given in Table 6.

SUMMARY

Many aspects of both rural and urban Sonoran life, including food consumption patterns, can be seen as related to the distinct culture that has developed there as a result of its distance from major Mexican population centers and proximity to those of the United States. While much of the surface level appearances of life in Sonora suggest that influences from the United States predominate (those Westinghouse, side-by-side refrigerator/freezers with automatic ice dispensers, and jars of U.S. mayonnaise become etched in one's mind, as does the familiarity of Sonorans with Tucson's shopping malls) examination of the lives and food use patterns of families with American wives reveals the extent to which the underlying pattern of life in Sonora is distinctly Mexican. The descriptive information about the food consumption patterns of each of the sample groups covered in this chapter will serve as the basis for the comparisons of the roles of key variables in affecting food consumption patterns which follow in Chapter 3.

CHAPTER 3

Trickling it In
Variables Affecting Amount of Available Income

INTRODUCTION

This chapter discusses the effects on food consumption of a number of variables which act by affecting the amount of available income of a household. These variables include rural to urban migration, income, women's roles, household size and intrahousehold distribution of food, and subsistence pattern.

RURAL TO URBAN MIGRATION

As discussed in Chapter 1, rural to urban migration may be associated with changes in food consumption patterns. This section examines the extent to which rural and urban patterns vary in ways which lead to a nutritional impact, and how the migrants compare with their rural cousins and urban neighbors. The groups least likely to be at nutritional risk are considered, as is information on food habits which explains this decreased risk.

On the basis of prices I recorded in the spring of 1982, the same market basket of food cost 9% more in Hermosillo than in Arroyo Lindo. However, much of this difference is due to the lower cost of the range-fed meat that is consumed in Arroyo Lindo. This type of meat is available in Hermosillo, though not at the Gigante supermarket where the rest of the urban prices were recorded. Therefore, it can be assumed that any food price differences between Arroyo Lindo and Hermosillo are insignificant. With the exception of two born in the city households (who paid 400 and 1800 pesos/month rent), all lower income households in the sample owned their own homes. Therefore, it can be assumed that there are no significant differences between Arroyo Lindo and Hermosillo in terms of percentage of household income spent on rent.

Examining first the households of lower household incomes, the migrants appear to consume the best diets (Table 8), having the highest consumption of all food types for which the groups differ significantly except for eggs and meat. The rural pattern is one of higher egg consumption, and lower dairy and meat consumption, while for those born in the city, vegetable, egg, and miscellaneous – MISC – (high energy, low nutrient foods such as soft drinks, chips, and candy) consumption are the lowest; total meat consumption is highest, as is consumption of meat at home (as opposed to meat consumed away from home). Differences by sample group of households with lower household incomes are fewer than among households of higher household incomes. Among the latter households, differences in food consumption among sample groups are seen for all food groups except alcohol; the rich differ more by group than do the poor (Table 8). Even at higher household incomes, Arroyo Lindo bean, egg and grain consumption is the highest, indicating that this is a rural pattern, independent of income. Urban patterns stress greater use of fruit, vegetables, dairy and meat, and decreased use of beans, eggs, grains, and MISC. The migrants follow the urban pattern for fruit, dairy, eggs, and meat; they follow the rural pattern for MISC. For vegetables, beans, and grains they have partially adopted the urban pattern; for potatoes they establish their own pattern, exceeding those of Arroyo Lindo and those born in the city. Note that regardless of income, dairy consumption is lowest in Arroyo

Table 8. Food Consumption of Individuals in Sample Groups (Mean Daily Servings)

	Lower Income Households				
	Arroyo Lindo	Migrants	Urban-Born		
Food	N = 135 15 HH	N = 88 9 HH	N = 84 18 HH		
Type	Mean	Mean	Mean	F	p*
Fruit	0.6	0.6	0.4	2.37	n.s.
Veg	0.7	0.8	0.5	5.12	<0.01
Beans	2.2	2.1	1.8	2.18	n.s.
Dairy	0.8	1.3	1.1	3.46	<0.05
Eggs	1.1	0.9	0.8	6.04	<0.01
Grains	7.1	6.6	6.0	2.58	n.s.
Misc	1.3	1.7	1.0	10.25	<0.01
Pot	0.5	0.5	0.4	2.07	n.s.
Meat	0.7	1.1	1.2	10.64	<0.01
Alc	0.1	0.1	0.2	0.33	n.s.

	Higher Income Households				
	Arroyo Lindo	Migrants	Urban-Born		
	N = 63 5 HH	N = 78 11 HH	N = 71 20 HH		
	Mean	Mean	Mean		
Fruit	0.6	1.1	1.1	4.00	<0.05
Veg	0.9	1.0	1.2	4.37	<0.05
Beans	1.1	0.8	0.6	10.25	<0.001
Dairy	0.6	1.6	1.8	21.98	<0.001
Eggs	1.1	0.8	0.9	3.81	<0.05
Grains	5.4	5.0	4.4	2.98	n.s.
Misc	1.3	1.7	0.8	15.61	<0.001
Pot	0.3	0.4	0.3	2.86	n.s.
Meat	1.5	2.1	1.9	5.56	<0.01
Alc	0.2	0.3	0.1	1.60	n.s.

* two-tailed; HH = Household.
Serving Units: Fruit – 1/2 c juice or cooked/canned or 1 medium piece; Vegetable – 1/2 c juice or cooked/canned or 3/4 c raw; Beans – 1/2 c cooked; Dairy – 1 c milk or 1 c plain yogurt or 1 1/3 oz. aged cheese; Eggs – 1 medium egg; Grains – 1 slice bread or 3/4 c cooked cereal, spaghetti, noodles; Misc – 1 soft drink (473 ml) or 1 small package potato chips, etc. or 1 medium sized candy bar or 1 c Kool-Aid; Potato – 1 medium; Meat – 2 to 3 oz. cooked meat/fish; Alcohol – 1 can beer or 1 mixed drink or 1/2 c wine.

Lindo, whose economy is based on raising dairy cattle and producing cheese.

In households of lower household incomes, there is a trend toward less planting of fruit trees among those born in the city (Table 6), perhaps due to the fact that in Arroyo Lindo there is a set rate for water – it is not metered. However, the migrants have more fruit trees than do those born in the city – even though both groups are paying similarly high rates for water. Differences in chicken ownership are also not significant, but a similar persistence of the rural pattern is seen among the migrants. Thus, lowest amounts of home production of eggs and fruit are characteristic of lower income households of those born in the city, in contrast to the patterns of Arroyo Lindo and of the migrants.

Among households of higher household incomes, the migrants conform to the urban pattern of fewer fruit trees, while all of the Arroyo Lindo households planted fruit trees. A similar pattern of significant differences is seen for chicken ownership. Therefore, with regard to home production, at lower household incomes, the migrant pattern is intermediate between that of Arroyo Lindo and that of those born in the city, but at higher household incomes, migrant behavior is almost identical to that of those born in the city.

At lower household incomes, breakfast patterns do not vary significantly by sample group. For households of higher incomes, use of meat at breakfast is most common in Arroyo Lindo; use of bread is most common among those born in the city. At lower household incomes, lunch for the rural household is most commonly a *sopa* or *caldo*; the migrants eat a similar meal, though more often with meat; those born in the city tend towards just a *sopa*. This pattern may be due to the cost of fuel; *sopa* cooks faster than *caldo*. Due to the high cost of cooking gas, in Arroyo Lindo a *caldo* is usually cooked on a wood store; firewood is free for the gathering. The migrants, many of whom still have land, and all of whom have relatives in Arroyo Lindo, may tend to have greater access to free firewood than do their urban born neighbors. At higher household incomes, the rural lunch tends to be a *sopa* and main dish; the migrants eat a one dish meal (similar to that of the lower income migrants); those born in the city eat a *sopa* and main dish, sometimes including vegetables, and less frequently including soft drinks. The evening meal for rural households of lower household incomes is usually a combination of beans, cheese, fried potatoes, and eggs; the migrants continue this pattern, with increased use of meat; those born in the city eat a similar evening meal, though with increased use of leftovers and sandwiches. Among households of higher household incomes, the rural and migrant evening meals are similar to those of the relevant households of lower household incomes. Those born in the city eat similar foods to those of the lower household incomes, with the major change being less use of beans.

Use of one pot meals is less frequent for those born in the city of higher household incomes, and dislike of one pot meals is cited by only those born in the city (at both income levels). At the same time, there is more focus on the nutritional value of one pot meals among those born in the city of higher household incomes. The explanation of this pattern of the simultaneous dislike and valuing of one pot meals may lie in their low prestige value among those born in the city, but they are used nevertheless by wives of higher household incomes as a means of encouraging vegetable consumption by hiding the vegetables among other foods. (The hidden vegetables may in turn further contribute to the dislike of these dishes). At lower household incomes, bread is second in use to tortillas only among those born in the city. This may again relate to access to firewood (tortillas are usually made on wood stoves) as well as to the higher prestige of bread in the urban areas. Tortilla use continues high among rural households of higher incomes. The migrants use predominantly tortillas, with some use of rice, pastas and bread. Those born in the city favor bread and potatoes almost as much as tortillas.

Rural to Urban Migration – Summary

Migrant food patterns vary by income and do not consistently follow either those of Arroyo Lindo or those people born in the city, but it would be very difficult to blame increased nutritional problems in the urban areas on the migrants. The data presented here suggest that the greatest problems would be found in those born in the city, followed by those in Arroyo Lindo. Particularly at lower household incomes, where nutritional problems would be expected, the migrants have retained some nutritionally positive rural patterns, including a more nutritious midday meal (*caldo* vs. *sopa*), as well as some rural economic patterns that affect available income and diet, including increased ownership of fruit trees and chickens (the products of which are generally not sold), and increased use of homemade tortillas (which may be less expensive than bread – in money, though not in time). Thus, the pattern of positive selectivity among rural-urban migrants suggested by the income and educational level data discussed in Chapter 2, is also seen in their food consumption patterns. This positive selectivity among lower household income migrants is noted not only in relation to place of origin (Arroyo Lindo), but also with regard to place of destination (Hermosillo). These findings, however, relate to a situation in which there was a change in neither subsistence pattern nor in availability of foods associated with the migration that took place.

INCOME

The role of income in food consumption patterns has been included to some extent in the previous discussions of the food consumption patterns of each of the sample groups and the extent to which they differ. As such, this section will focus on differences in dietary intakes based on income at the level of the total sample as well as on aspects of household economics and the way in which these factors affect intakes. Key issues addressed are: the way in which income allocation decisions are made, the extent to which different sources of income lead to different nutritional outcomes, and the role of the wife's economic activity on household dietary patterns.

Dietary intakes by income level are presented in Table 9. As house hold income increases, consumption of fruit, vegetables, dairy, and meat increases; consumption of beans, grains, and potatoes decreases. It is interesting that, contrary, to the beliefs of people of higher household incomes, who tend to feel that the poor drink up all of their incomes, there are no significant differences in reported alcohol consumption by household income. However, relative to their household income, the poor may be spending a higher percentage of their household income on alcohol than

Table 9. Food Consumption at Higher and Lower Incomes (Mean Daily Servings)

Food Type	Lower Income N* = 307 42 HH Mean	Higher Income N* = 211 36 HH Mean	F	p**
Fruit	0.6	1.0	18.41	< 0.000
Vegetables	0.7	1.0	28.01	< 0.000
Beans	2.0	0.8	111.83	< 0.000
Dairy	1.0	1.4	11.06	< 0.001
Eggs	0.9	0.9	0.26	n.s.
Grains	6.7	4.9	40.12	< 0.000
Misc	1.3	1.3	0.36	n.s.
Potatoes	0.5	0.3	15.54	< 0.000
Meat	1.0	1.9	91.88	< 0.000
Alcohol	0.1	0.2	3.58	n.s.

* Weighted N; ** two-tailed; HH = Household.
Serving Units: Fruit – 1/2 c juice or cooked/canned or 1 medium piece; Vegetable – 1/2 c juice or cooked/canned or 3/4 raw; Beans – 1/2 c cooked; Dairy – 1 c milk or 1 c plain yogurt or 1 1/3 oz. aged cheese; Eggs – 1 medium egg; Grains – 1 slice bread or 3/4 c cooked cereal, spaghetti, noodles; Misc – 1 soft drink (473 ml) or 1 small package potato chips, etc. or 1 medium sized candy bar or 1 c Kool-aid; Potato – 1 medium; Meat – 2 to 3 oz. cooked meat or fish; Alcohol – 1 can beer or 1 mixed drink or 1/2 c wine.

are the rich – unless the latter are tending to consume more expensive types of alcohol to the exclusion of less expensive types.

At all income levels the husband's income is generally used for the main household expenses. Lupita, for example, was adamant that it was her husband who supported the family. In households with more than one income, at lower household incomes this allocation is usually decided by the husband among the migrants and those born in the city, and in Arroyo Lindo by the husband and wife (50%) or by the husband (50%). At higher household incomes, in Arroyo Lindo and among those born in the city, the decision as to how the husband's income is spent is made by the husband and wife; among the migrants, it is the decision of the husband. In households of lower household incomes with more than one income, an increase in the husband's income would most likely be spent as follows: Arroyo Lindo, on savings; among those born in the city, on clothes or bills; migrants, on house improvements, food, savings, or keeping up with inflation. Among households of lower household incomes, no Arroyo Lindo household would use the increased income for food, whereas 25% of the migrant households and 17% of the households of those born in the city in which there was more than one income would do so. At higher household incomes, an increase in the husband's income would be used for house improvements in Arroyo Lindo, savings for the migrants, and house improvements or savings for those born in the city.

In most cases wives' incomes are used for general household expenses or food, as was the case in Dora's household. How the wife's income will be spent is decided by the wife generally, although in some Arroyo Lindo households of higher household incomes and among those born in the city of higher household incomes the decision is made by the husband and wife. At lower household incomes, an increase in the wife's income would most likely be spent on children's clothing in Arroyo Lindo, or on house improvements by the migrants, and on house improvements, childrens' clothing or wife's personal expenses by those born in the city. The only households that indicated that an increase in the wife's income would be spent on food were in Arroyo Lindo and represented 20% of the households in which the wives had their own sources of income. At higher household incomes, an increase in the wife's income would most likely be used for children's clothing in Arroyo Lindo, on personal expenses by the migrants, and on house improvements, savings, or charity by those born in the city.

In those households where children or other relatives are working, the pattern in Sonora is that these other workers generally contribute only a portion of their earnings to the husband or the wife of the household, retaining the rest of their income to dispose of as they choose. For example, Maria has three adult children living in her household, all of whom are employed, and who all contribute a portion of their earnings to their mother. At lower household incomes, the decision regarding how these incomes are allocated is made by the husband in Arroyo Lindo, and by the other wage earners themselves among the migrants and those born in the city. For those of higher household incomes, the decision is made by the other wage earner in Arroyo Lindo; by him/her or by the wife and husband among the migrants; and by the wife, the wife and husband, or the other wage earners among those born in the city. At lower household incomes, increased income for these other family members would result in a larger contribution to the husband or wife in Arroyo Lindo and among those born in the city; among the migrants this pattern is one of several that are fol- lowed. The other possibility is that all the increase would be used by the other wage earner for personal expenses such as clothes. At higher household incomes, such increases would be spent on the other wage earners' school costs among those of Arroyo Lindo and the migrants, among those born in the city, all of the increase would be contributed to the household.

Major decisions on expenditures such as rent or house payments are usually made by the husband. Food expenditures are generally controlled by the wife, or she has considerable input into those decisions. Of the groups studied, the wife has the least input in lower household income Arroyo Lindo households. Decisions on other major purchases are most commonly made by the husband.

A general increase in household income – with the particular source unspecified, or in households where there is only one income – would be spent by households of lower household incomes generally on house improvements, furniture, or televisions. The only households who indicated that they would use an increase to purchase food was one of the Arroyo Lindo households. The households of higher household incomes would spend such an increase on appliances (such as washing machines, or kitchen sinks) in Arroyo Lindo, on savings or children's educations among the migrants, and on house improvements, furniture, and televisions among those born in the city.

If provided with increased income which could only be spent on food, 21% of households of lower household incomes responded that they desired no changes in their diets and/or would try to keep the money to spend on other things (although this sentiment was least common among those born in the city). The women often insisted that they would find ways to keep the money, but spend it on things other than food. Of those who desired changes in their diets, most wished to purchase more meat or better cuts of meat. At higher household incomes, 40% desired no changes (although this feeling was highest among the migrants). Those in Arroyo Lindo wished to buy more of everything while the migrants said they would buy more meat or better cuts of meat, and those born in the city desired more fruits, vegetables, and/or juices.

In the case of having less income available for food, the households of lower household incomes in Arroyo Lindo indicated they would decrease use of all, especially of pastas and beans, substituting cheaper meats (such as liver or soup bones), and rice, potatoes, and tortillas. The migrants and those born in the city would cut back on all, and especially on meat, substituting non-meat protein sources (such as beans). Arroyo Lindo households of higher household incomes would reduce use of snack foods, candy, and soft drinks. The migrants would cut back on all, especially canned and convenience foods. For those born in the city, cuts would be made in purchases of all, except vegetables and starches, which would be increased.

The rampant inflation typical of Mexico in 1982 was noted most at lower household incomes. The effects of inflation were ameliorated for more of lower household income urban born and of higher household income migrants than for any of the other groups, primarily via salary increases for the husbands, or price increases by those with small businesses. Forty-one percent of households of lower household income indicated that they had decreased spending on food; this was also true for 19% of households of higher household incomes. Other changes caused by inflation were reductions in clothes purchases by households of lower household incomes, and reductions in spending on clothes, travel and recreation, and furniture and appliances among households of higher household incomes.

Income – Summary

Thus, among households of lower household incomes in Sonora, dietary changes are not at the top of the household priorities list for how to spend increased income. Further, changes in diet are most likely to result if the additional income is earned by the husband or wife, as opposed to other working members of the household. If forced to spend more money on food, most would increase consumption of meat – a food of high prestige value. Inflation has caused a reduction in food expenditures for many households, generally involving reduced consumption of meat, starches, vegetables, shortening, and dairy products. It is interesting to note the extent to which these ethnographic data parallel those of the dietary intakes. As household incomes increase (Table 9), so also does consumption of fruit, vegetables, dairy, and meat. Meat and fruit consumption increase the most as income increases, and meat is the food which households of lower household incomes stress they would like to consume in greater quantities.

WOMEN'S ROLES

As discussed above, the ethnographic data indicate that husband and wife's incomes and salary increases are more likely to affect household dietary intake than are those of other household workers. Therefore, raising household income by raising the income of either the husband or the wife would have a greater nutritional impact than providing employment for children or other household members. However, a potential conflict between childcare and women's work may exist. This issue can be evaluated by analysis of the dietary intake data, focusing on the dietary effect of working and economically active wives. Working wives are defined as those who receive payment for their labors. Economically active wives are · those who contribute labor besides that of housework, but who do not receive a separate paycheck for their work. A typical example of this is a wife who works in a family business. Ana, a migrant wife, serves as the secretary for her husband's business, which operates out of their home, but receives no salary; she was categorized as an economically active wife.

Mean per capita annual household income does not differ significantly whether or not the wife is employed. However, significant differences in mean daily food consumption of fruit and dairy are noted between these two types of households, with those of working wives consuming less of each. No significant mean per capita annual income differences were found between households of economically active wives and those in which the wife is not economically active. However, households with economically active wives consume significantly fewer grains and potatoes.

The income allocation patterns discussed above suggest that in households where there are multiple workers (other than the husband and wife), there is likely to be a difference between total household income and total household income which is available for household expenses, including household food, or available income. While total and available incomes differ significantly for both types of households, available income drops much more in households where there are multiple workers (Table 10). Available income was calculated by considering as part of household income only that income which is contributed by a worker to one of the household heads to be used for household expenses. Incomes of other · household wage earners may be used for their own food, i.e. food purchased and consumed outside the household. But this type of behavior has little effect on household food supplies as a whole, other than not having to feed that person that meal.

Food consumption patterns for these two groups (Table 11) are significantly different for several food types. Multiple worker households consume less total fruit, dairy and MISC, and more beans and alcohol. These

Table 10. Mean Annual Per Capita Household Income

Household Work Structure	N*	Total Income	Available Income
Only head(s) of household economically active	45		
Mean		50,495	47,339
SD		33,711	33,812
t	1.95		
df	44		
p (one-tailed)	< 0.05		
Multiple Workers	32		
Mean		52,167	36,381
SD		29,219	27,226
t	4.03		
df	31		
p (one-tailed)	< 0.000		

* Weighted N.

Table 11. Mean Daily Per Capita Food Consumption and Household Structure

Food Type	Only Head(s) of Economically Active N* = 253 46 HH Mean	Multiple Workers N* = 265 30 HH Mean	T	p**
Fruit	0.9	0.6	3.75	< 0.001
Veg	0.8	0.8	−0.42	n.s.
Beans	1.4	1.7	−3.03	< 0.01
Dairy	1.5	0.9	5.76	< 0.001
Eggs	1.0	0.9	1.13	n.s.
Grains	5.8	6.1	−0.79	n.s.
Misc	1.4	1.2	2.23	< 0.05
Pot	0.4	0.5	−1.63	n.s.
Meat	1.4	1.3	0.46	n.s.
Alc	0.1	0.2	−2.48	< 0.05

* Weighted N; ** two-tailed; HH = Household.
Serving Units: Fruit – 1/2 c juice or cooked/canned or 1 medium piece; Vegetable – 1/2 c juice or cooked/canned or 3/4 c raw; Beans – 1/2 c cooked; Dairy – 1 c milk or 1 c plain yogurt or 1 1/3 oz. aged cheese; Eggs – 1 medium egg; Grains – 1 slice bread or 3/4 c cooked cereal, spaghetti, noodles; Misc – 1 soft drink (473 ml) or 1 small package potato chips, etc. or 1 medium sized candy bar or 1 c Kool-Aid; Potato – 1 medium; Meat – 2 to 3 oz. cooked meat/fish; Alcohol – 1 can beer or 1 mixed drink or 1/2 c wine.

differences correspond to available income differences, rather than house-hold income differences. It therefore appears that collection of data on both total household income and available income will increase the accu-racy of future studies of the relationship between income and dietary ade-quacy in this region.

The negative effects on dietary intakes of working and economically active wives can be explained by the extent to which they occur in multi-ple worker households (Table 12). This pattern points out the importance of using available income in calculations – otherwise the impact on food consumption patterns of working and economically active wives would be incorrectly interpreted. What appear to be the effects working or economi-cally active wives are actually those of lower available incomes, related to household structural pattern.

The operation of this pattern can be illustrated by considering the effect on household dietary intake of an economically active wife while control-ling for household structure. In the case of multiple worker households of lower available incomes, such as that of Elena and Juan (mother and father) and their three working children in their twenties, the presence of an economically active wife results in increased consumption of fruit, eggs, and meat, and decreased use of dairy and potatoes. For households in which the only workers are the household head(s), such as that of Tonia and Raoul (mother and father) and their six school aged children, the pres-ence of an economically active wife results in an increase in fruit, veg-etable, dairy, and MISC consumption, and a decrease in use of beans, eggs, and grains. At higher available incomes, there is a dietary change which focuses mostly in changes in sources of calories, with a greater improve-ment seen for the households in which there are not multiple workers.

There may be a relationship between place of birth, income level, and whether a wife will be economically active. Economic activity among

Table 12. Household Structure and Wives Work/Economic Activity

Wife's Status	Only Head(s) of Household Economically Active	Multiple Workers
Working Wife		
N* = 21 Households	38%	63%
Economically Active Wife		
N* = 34 Households	52%	48%

N* = Weighted N.

wives seems highest in all rural and migrant households, regardless of income, and in higher household income women who were born in the city Table 13. Some of this pattern may be due to sampling error; as discussed in Chapter 2, random sampling was not used. However, in Arroyo Lindo, the desired number of households were selected by identifying households with the required characteristics; no problem was encountered in doing so and including households with economically active wives. The migrant sample of the siblings or close relatives of those in Arroyo Lindo also produced a large percentage of households with economically active wives. In Hermosillo, the same types of selection techniques produced very few households of economically active wives at lower available incomes levels.

If this pattern is, as I strongly suspect, not completely due to sampling error, it may relate to the low prestige accorded to women's work. Among lower income urbanites, the women who work tend to be either single,

Table 13. Relationship Between Income Level, Economic Activity of Wife and Group

Group	Number of Economically Active Wives	Percentage of Economically Active wives
Arroyo Lindo – Lower Income Households (N = 15 Households; 135 Individuals)	8	53%
Arroyo Lindo – Higher Income Households (N = 5 Households; 63 Individuals)	3	60%
Migrants – Lower Income Households (N = 9 Households; 88 Individuals)	7	77%
Migrants – Higher Income Households (N = 11 Households; 78 Individuals)	3	27%
Urban-Born – Lower Income Households (N = 18 Households; 84 Individuals)	3	17%
Urban-Born – Higher Income Households (N = 20 Households; 71 Individuals)	9	45%

Per Capita. Income Categories: Lower income 0 – 49,000; Higher income 49,001 + (In pesos: 40 pesos = $1.00).

divorced, abandoned, or those who are unwed mothers; they are often employed in occupations of very low prestige, for example, as maids. Women born in the city may therefore feel that if they choose to be economically active, it somehow implies that they either have no man to support them, or that their husband is unable or unwilling to do so. In urban higher income groups, women's work tends to be invisible. It often takes place in the home; Sandra bakes cakes in her kitchen and sells them. If their work is visible, working women in this group tend to work in professions of high prestige; Dora directs a research institute. The migrant wives, on the other hand, tend to continue the rural pattern of high rates of economic activity among wives. Natalia has a taco stand; Marta operates a *tienda*; Rosa is a seamstress. These women are either unaware of urban prestige sanctions, or their desire to get ahead causes them to ignore such sanctions.

Sampling error in this study is suggested, in that data from a study conducted by the Centro de Investigacíon en Alimentacíon y Desarollo in Hermosillo of a randomly selected 0.1% sample (500 households) of the population of Hermosillo (using sociological survey methodology) does not indicate different rates of employment (as opposed to economic activity, which is what I have emphasized above) among rural and urban-born women. But it was my experience that women who work at home and/or part-time frequently do not consider themselves to be employed. This is often also true of women who are economically active but who do not receive a separate paycheck. On numerous occasions, a woman's status as economically active was revealed to me only accidentally after several visits to the household, and many direct questions about the employment status of each person in the household. Further, women born in the city may feel that admitting economic activity to a relative stranger doing a one visit survey implies something about the state of their marriage or lack thereof. Clearly then, the extent to which rural and urban-born women differ in rates of economic activity is yet to be established.

Thus, regardless of the extent to which there are differences in economic activity of wives by sample group, the nutritionally positive effects of economic activity of wives remain; the dietary intake data again confirm the pattern suggested by the ethnographic data. Returning to the ethnographic data base suggests explanations for dietary patterns observed. Conflicts with childcare do not seem to be a serious problem; many of the economically active wives are involved in the informal sector of the economy where they have a great deal of control over their working hours; in many cases they are working in their homes. Further, much of the work of these women is part-time. Among non-migrants of lower household incomes, wives tend to be economically active for fewer then 30 hours per week.

Among households of higher households income, wives in all sample groups tend to be economically active for fewer then 30 hours per week.

With regard to allocation of income, only 12% of the non-working wives at lower household incomes felt that if they were working they would spend more money on food (the trend to spend more money on food was highest among those born in the city and lowest in Arroyo Lindo). At higher household incomes, only 17% felt they would spend more money on food if they were working (with the trend highest among the migrants and lowest in Arroyo Lindo). Of lower household income working wives, 27% felt that they were spending more on food because they were working (highest among the migrants and lowest among those born in the city). Of higher household income working wives, 17% felt that their working led to increased expenditures on food (highest in Arroyo Lindo and lowest among the migrants). One reason why more money may be spent on food in households of economically active wives is that the economically active wife may have more power in deciding the percentage of household income which is to be spent on food. While the differences are not significant, there is a tendency for economically active wives to have greater involvement in this aspect of household economics. However, many of the wives did stress the fact that other expenditures, such as children's clothing were viewed as a more important way of spending their earnings than was spending more money on food.

There were no significant differences in amount of time spent cooking by economically active wives and non-economically active wives. However, the non-economically active wives of lower household incomes did spend slightly more time cooking (3.2 hours/day vs. 2.9 hours/day). While the economically active wives have changed little in the amount of time they allocate to cooking for their families, time is an important concern to them. Many working wives indicated that their increased tiredness and decreased time to relax were the main effects of their working. Of those for whom time was the key factor in decisions about food consumption (only 9% of the total sample), 5 out of 6 were economically active wives. Of those wives for whom convenience was the key factor (5% of the total sample) 3 out of 4 were economically active wives. In contrast, many of the non-economically active wives tended to choose "money" as the key factor. This concern with time and convenience among economically active wives results in a tendency toward increased eating out only for households at higher household incomes. Therefore, time pressure is most intense for economically active wives in households of lower household incomes.

The factor of increased expenditures on food (perhaps due to increased power in household income allocation decisions), with little or no decrease in time spent cooking or in quality of child care, may explain to some extent why wives' economic activity has a positive effect on household dietary intake. Additional factors are suggested by comments by several of the women during the ethnographic interview. They noted that in many households the common pattern is for the husband to give his wife a certain amount of money every two weeks to cover household expenses. If she runs out and needs more, she either asks her husband for more, or makes do with what she has. Lola, a non-working wife who was born in the city said that when she had unexpected expenses such as children's school books, medicine, or unexpectedly high utility bills, she simply reduced spending on food. She saw her role as being one of a capable household manager and may have been reluctant to ask her husband for additional money as that would indicate her failure in carrying out the duties of her role (Roldan [1988] reports a similar pattern in Mexico City). Working wives would not have this problem, as they could simply make up the short-fall themselves. The working wives, as well as the economically active wives impressed me as being more independent and assertive individuals (which may be why they chose to be economically active). It is possible that these women would be less reluctant to approach their husbands for additional money, especially as the women and their husbands were aware that the wives were contributing labor above and beyond their duties as housewives. Economic activity on the part of the wife, may, therefore, actually help these women to better fulfill their traditional roles as good mothers and wives, as they are better able to feed their families.

Women's Roles – Summary

When household type is controlled, economic activity of wives has a positive nutritional effect on household diet. This is due to few conflicts with childcare, and other traditional responsibilities of the wife (including cooking), as well as patterns of allocation of wives' earnings. Economic activity seems to be associated with rural traditions, and is seen most in rural and migrant women; it may be of low prestige in urban areas.

INTRAHOUSEHOLD DISTRIBUTION OF FOOD

Increasing a household's food supply affects nutritional status only if the additional food is channeled to those household members who are at most nutritional risk. This section will address the extent to which larger household size is an important factor contributing to nutritional problems in the populations under study.

Preferential access by the older age groups is often thought to explain nutritional problems that seem to correlate with household size. The data from this study largely corroborate the reported relationship of household size to food consumption. Households smaller than or equal to the regional mean of 6 persons per household (Valencia 1980; 1981) consume per capita greater amounts of all food types (for which there are significant differences), except beans and grains (Table 14). This pattern is more likely due to the effects of income than household size. Table 15 shows a comparison

Table 14. A Comparison of Mean Daily Per Capita Servings in Small and Large Households

Food Type	Small HH Mean N*= 165 Indiv. (36 HH)	Large HH Mean N*= 354 Indiv. (42 HH)	t	p
Fruit	1.2	0.5	6.44	< 0.0000
Veg	0.9	0.8	2.76	< 0.0000
Beans	1.0	1.8	6.29	< 0.0000
Dairy	1.4	1.0	3.21	< 0.0000
Eggs	1.0	0.9	2.54	< 0.0112
Grains	5.4	6.2	2.80	< 0.0052
Misc	1.2	1.3	0.77	n.s.
Pot	0.4	0.4	1.34	n.s.
Meat	1.7	1.2	4.95	< 0.0000
Alc	0.1	0.2	0.71	n.s.

N* = Weighted N; HH = Household.

Table 15. A Comparison of Household and Available Per Capita Income Per Household Size

Household size	N*	Total Income	Available Income
Small households (≤6)	35		
Mean		52,474	49,255
SD		36,238	36,859
t −0.48			
df 66			
p ns			
Larger Households (>6)	42		
Mean		48,828	36,317
SD		29,003	25,987
t −01.76			
df 61			
p ≤0.05			

N* = Weighted N.

of household and available incomes by household size. Household and available incomes are not significantly different for the smaller households, whereas they do differ significantly for the larger households (using a one-tailed test, since available income cannot be expected to be greater than household income.)

Dependency ratios (the ratio of workers to dependents) are mentioned in the literature (Chaudhury 1984; Marchione 1980) as being a factor that may also be of importance in explaining the food consumption problems observed in larger households. However, in this case, no significant differences were observed in dependency ratios between the larger and smaller households. The larger households do not have more dependent children; they have more adults (and young adults). Therefore, these households have more adults to be economically active.

The smaller households are structurally different from the larger households in that the latter tend to be of the multiple worker type (Table 16). This structural difference will have the effect of making per capita household and available incomes in the smaller households more similar than is the case in the larger households. The different structure of the larger households (and its critical implication for income allocation) has the effect of making per capita household and available incomes more different than is the case in the smaller households.

In households of lower per capita available incomes – those that would be predicted to be at greater nutritional risk – per capita food consumption of the smaller households differs significantly from that of the larger households for vegetables, MISC, meat, and alcohol, with the smaller

Table 16. The Association between Household Size and Household Structure

Household Size	Only Heads of Household Economically Active		Multiple Workers		N*
	Number	%	Number	%	
Small Households (⩽6)	30	85	6	15	36
Large Households (>6)	16	38	26	63	42
				Total	78
X^2 16.399					
df 1					
p ⩽0.0001					

N* = Weighted N.

households consuming greater per capita amounts of these foods. Therefore, the problems of the larger household appear to be related to its lower per capita available income and thus, lower per capita consumption of almost all food types.

The connection of these factors with nutritional status can be seen by examining these patterns in the Arroyo Lindo households, for which all children of sample households 13 years old or less were weighed and measured and compared to the Ramos Galvan Standards (1975). These standards use ratios of height, weight and age to establish the nutritional status of an individual. If a household had more than one child who was at least 1st degree malnourished in terms of height for age, the household was classified as "stunted." Households with more than one child who was at least 1st degree malnourished in terms of weight for height, were classified as "wasted." The remainder of the households were considered as "normal."

For the Arroyo Lindo households, as in the total sample, per capita available incomes were lower for larger households, as was per capita dietary intake. The household structural pattern in which there are multiple workers in addition to the household heads was also more common in the larger Arroyo Lindo households. When the stunted households were compared with the normal ones, household size was significantly different in the stunted households (Table 17).

Stunted households were also more likely to be of the multiple worker type (Table 18). A number of Laura's children were categorized as "stunted"; her household contains four workers, herself, her husband, and two adult children. This pattern, as in the sample as a whole, relates to available

Table 17. A Comparison of Household Size of "Stunted" and "Normal" Arroyo Lindo Households

Household Size	Stunted Households $N = 10$	Normal Households $N = 10$
Mean	10.3	6.0
SD	3.1	2.3
t 3.55		
df 16.75		
p $\leqslant 0.01$		

Note: The magnitude of the differences in households sizes far surpasses that which would be due to the bias introduced by the methods of classification of the households (i.e., the way in which non-normal households were defined makes it somewhat more likely that a larger household – ones with more children – will have the chance to "express" malnourished children, and therefore not be classified as "normal" than will a smaller household).

Table 18. Household Structure of "Stunted" and "Normal" Arroyo Lindo Households

Type of Household		Only Heads of Households Economically Active		Multiple Workers	
		Number	%	Number	%
Stunted	N = 10	4	40	6	60
Normal	N = 10	9	90	1	10
X²	6.8				
df	1				
p	≤ 0.01				

Table 19. A Comparison of Household and Available Per Capita Income in "Stunted" and "Normal" Arroyo Lindo Households

Household Classification		Household Income	Available Income
Stunted	N = 10		
Mean		34,589	24,738
SD		21,495	15,748
t	− 0.56		
df	17.99		
p	ns		
Normal	N = 10		
Mean		39,962	38,818
SD		21,057	21,458
t	− 1.67		
df	16.51		
p	ns		

incomes (Table 19), which drop greatly below those of household incomes only for the "stunted" households. While these differences are not statistically significant for this small subsample, the pattern does seem to follow that of the larger sample (Table 15) for which significant relationships were observed.

Patterns of food consumption for this subsample also seem to follow that observed in the larger sample (Table 14). Food consumption was lower for the "stunted" households as compared with the "normal" households for all food types for which there were significant differences – fruit, dairy, and potatoes (Table 20). Similar patterns were seen when the "wasted" households were compared with the normal households.

Table 20. A Comparison of Mean Daily Per Capita Servings in Arroyo Lindo "Stunted" and "Normal" Households

Food Type	Stunted HH Mean N=98 individuals (10 HH)	Normal HH Mean N=52 individuals (10 HH)	t	p
Fruit	0.4	1.1	−3.14	<0.01
Veg	0.7	0.8	−0.39	n.s.
Beans	1.7	2.1	−1.43	n.s.
Dairy	0.7	0.9	−1.11	n.s.
Eggs	1.0	1.2	−2.05	<0.05
Grains	6.5	6.6	−0.22	n.s.
MISC	1.2	1.4	−1.42	n.s.
Pot	0.4	0.6	−3.53	<0.01
Meat	0.9	1.0	−0.49	n.s.
Alc	0.2	0.2	−0.01	n.s.

HH = Household

Further evidence against the hypotheses that nutritional problems of the larger Arroyo Lindo households are due to competition between the young and the old is seen by comparing assessments of the weights of the husbands and wives (subjectively, the husbands and wives were categorized as normal, thin, fat) with the nutritional status of their children. In only one case was a "fat" husband or wife found in a household which had been categorized as anything other than "normal".

Intrahousehold Distribution of Food – Summary

These data suggest that the problems of large households may be related to the low available incomes characteristic of those situations. This pattern is related to the frequency with which larger households are of the multiple worker type, in which available incomes tend to be much lower than in households in which only the head(s) of household are working.

Subsistence Pattern

Differences in home gardening among the sample groups and the dietary changes as Arroyo Lindo shifted from a subsistence to a market economy have been previously discussed (this chapter and Chapter 2). This section will focus on a comparison of Arroyo Lindo with two other villages also involved in commercial ranching and agriculture. The factors that cause amounts of home production to vary will be examined, as will be the role of production for home consumption in avoiding nutritional problems.

Table 21. Dairy Cattle Ownership by Village

Village	Number of Cattle Owners	Percentage of Total Owners	Number of Dairy Cattle Owned	Average Head	% of Dairy Cattle Owned
Milpas Verdes:					
Ejido Members	16	31%	443	28	35
Private Owners	36	69%	771	21	64
Los Cerritos:					
Ejido Members	71	67%	1801	25	24
Private Owners	34	32%	5631	166	76
Arroyo Lindo:					
Ejido Members	29	21%	492	17 ⎫	53
Comunidad Members	99	71%	2809	28 ⎭	
Private Owners	12	9%	2953	246	47

The severe land problems in Arroyo Lindo, their relationship to the nutritional problems observed, and the claim made by everyone from Agrarian Reform officials to people in Arroyo Lindo that Arroyo Lindo had more land problems than other villages in the area, suggested that villages with fewer land problems should also have fewer nutritional problems. Thus, Arroyo Lindo, characterized by many problems over land and powerful enemies, was compared with Los Cerritos, which has many problems over land but fewer problems with large absentee owners, and Milpas Verdes, located between the two other villages (Figure 3). Only 12 km. from Arroyo Lindo, Milpas Verdes has exclusive use of water from a small nearby dam to irrigate its fields, in which cattle fodder, as well as other crops are grown.

All three villages have similar economies of cheese production. Intermarriage among the villages is frequent, as is visiting. The villages vary in relative degree of access to productive resources. As land quality may vary greatly, productive resources have been compared in terms of number of dairy cattle owned (Table 21) based on the 1981 livestock census. In Milpas Verdes, the relationships between control of productive resources (as measured by dairy cattle) and number of owners, is fairly equal, with ejido cattle owners (31% of total cattle owners) owning 36% of the cattle, and private cattle owners (69% of total cattle owners) owning 64% of the cattle. As we move to Los Cerritos and Arroyo Lindo, we see progressively more concentration of wealth in fewer hands.

By examining the private owners in terms of size of herds, it can be seen that the problem is even more serious (see Table 22). In Milpas

Table 22. Size of Herds of Private Owners

Group	Number	% of Total Private Owners
Milpas Verdes Private Owners		
0–49 dairy cattle	29	81
50–99 dairy cattle	6	17
100+ dairy cattle	1	3
Los Cerritos Private Owners		
0–49 dairy cattle	13	38
50–99 dairy cattle	8	24
100+ dairy cattle	13	38
Arroyo Lindo Private Owners		
0–49 dairy cattle	2	17
50–99 dairy cattle	1	8
100+ dairy cattle	9	75

Verdes, the private owners are, for the most part, small holders, as are 62% of the private holders in Los Cerritos. In Arroyo Lindo, however, only 25% of the private owners can be considered relatively small holders. Thus, in actuality, control of productive resources in that village is even more highly concentrated. Further, in Arroyo Lindo, it can be calculated that only about 56% of the households even own cattle, as opposed to about 91% in Los Cerritos and about 100% in Milpas Verdes.[1]

School-age children in the three villages were weighed and measured and their ages recorded (Table 23). To avoid encountering problems with adolescent growth spurts, only those students up to 10 years of age were included in the analysis. Following the advice of regional specialists in nutrition at the Centro de Investigacion en Alimentacion y Desarrollo in Hermosillo, the NCHS standards, which cover this age range, were used to analyze the anthropometric data. The results indicate that with regard to

Table 23. Anthropometric – Data NCHS Standards

		Arroyo Lindo		Los Cerritos		Milpas Verdas	
		Number	%	Number	%	Number	%
Height for Age							
Good Growth	>95%*	87	63	68	82	36	95
Poor Growth	<95%	51	37	15	18	2	5
Weight for Age							
Obese	>110%	19	14	20	24	17	45
Normal	90–110%	77	56	38	46	17	45
1st Degree Malnutrition	75–90%	37	27	25	30	4	11
2nd Degree Malnutrition	60–75%	5	4	0	0	0	0
3rd Degree Malnutrition	<60%	0	0	0	0	0	0
Weight for Height							
Obese	>110%	43	27	19	23	5	19
Normal	90–110%	111	69	61	73	19	70
Mild Malnutrition	85–90%	5	3	3	4	2	7
Moderate Malnutrition	75–85%	1	1	1	1	1	4
Severe Malnutrition	<75%	0	0%	0	0%	0	0%

* Reference values are the NCHS median values in the appropriate age, sex, and measurement categories based on the U.S. population (Hamill, Drizd, Johnson, Reed, Roche, and Moore 1979).

weight for age and height for age, there are different patterns of nutritional status in the three villages, with the children in Milpas Verdes the best nourished, and those of Arroyo Lindo at the other end of the continuum.

Subsistence Pattern – Summary

There seems to be a definite relationship between access to land (and therefore cattle ownership) and other productive resources (the irrigation system in Milpas Verdes), and degree of chronic mild to moderate malnutrition in school age children – the group who in this population have been identified as being at most risk (Valencia 1980). The irrigation system in Milpas Verdes apparently allows a greater amount of production for home consumption, as well as eliminating at least part of the necessity of buying cattle food. Both of these factors have the effect of raising available income (i.e., there is more money available for the purchasing of other foods). Further, given the type of flexible inputs to which Milpas Verdes has access (irrigation water), and fairly equitable division of other resources (dairy cattle), a conflict between adequate nutritional status and involvement in commercial ranching and agriculture does not seem to be inevitable.

CONCLUSIONS

The results of the analyses of this chapter point to available income as being a key factor affecting food consumption patterns. Household structure, working and economically active wives, and household size are important because of the extent to which they affect the amount of per capita available income. Lower household income migrant status has a positive effect on food consumption (as compared with the rural and urban-born lower household income households), due to household patterns and food habits of this group, many of which increase available income. Home production has an important positive effect on consumption patterns, and lack of access in some rural villages to key resources – land and water – necessary to enable home production as well as cattle raising, results in lower available income and is directly linked to nutritional problems.

Notes

1. These calculations were done using 1980 census figures for population and 1970 census figures for household size. For Milpas Verdes for which neither of

these were available, number of households was calculated on the basis of similar ratio of households to number of school children as in the other two villages. The figure used for household size was the average of those of the two villages for which data were available. These calculations assume only one cattle owner per household, which may or may not be true in all cases. However, lacking a complete census of cattle ownership, or lack thereof in each of the villages, these approximations do point to generally different patterns from village to village.

CHAPTER 4

Dishing it Out
Allocation of Available Income

INTRODUCTION

This chapter discusses the effects on food consumption of a number of variables which act by affecting how available income is allocated among competing wants and needs. These variables include prestige, ethnicity, desires for consumer goods, and nutritional knowledge.

PRESTIGE

The prestige value of certain foods – meat, bread, and *caldos* – and their role in affecting consumption patterns has been touched upon. This section expands on this discussion through an analysis of what rich and poor eat, as well as holiday foods, to understand their role as symbols of prestige in the various study populations.

At lower household incomes, those in Arroyo Lindo feel that the rich eat more meat, while the migrants felt that meat, chicken, fruits, vegetables and dairy products were used by the rich. Those born in the city generally agreed with this view, although many felt that the rich ate the same foods as they. At higher household incomes, those in Arroyo Lindo strongly felt that the rich ate worse than the poor. Higher household income migrants shared this view, although many stressed the variety of foods and increased meat used by the rich. Higher household income urban-born felt that use of increased meat, seafood, and products from the United States was typical of the rich.

It is interesting that the feeling that the rich ate worse than the poor was strongest at higher household incomes. Respondents had a variety of explanations for why the rich behaved in this manner. As Lilian put it, "the rich may not eat that well because they are stingy or spending money on things like cars. Those that have cars may be eating just beans." Maria stated that "the rich are always on diets, therefore they must eat less. She's always on a diet and he has ulcers." Elena observed that the rich often skip meals, often eating only at noon. Silva explained that "the rich don't like to cook, or they're very busy socializing." The patterning of these responses suggests that it may be not the poor who try to pull the rich down to their own level, but rather the upwardly mobile who seek, but have not yet achieved, the status of those who are considered to be of greater means.

Arroyo Lindo households of lower household incomes felt that the poor ate either just beans and tortillas, or gave a relatively accurate account of what the poor actually eat (beans, tortillas, *sopas*, potatoes, eggs, *caldos*). The migrants and those born in the city gave an accurate description of foods of the poor, or as Julia put it, "the poor eat as we do." However, Anita, a lower household income migrant women, felt that, "my children eat mostly beans and *sopas*, but they will grow up better than richer children. The children of the rich are 'weak.'" At higher household incomes there was also generally an accurate idea of the foods of the poor, although some of the migrants of higher household incomes felt that the poor ate as they did. Those born in the city tended most towards the stereotypical concept that the poor subsist on beans and tortillas to the exclusion of other foods.

Certain ways of eating also have prestige association. In Arroyo Lindo, it is considered correct in all households to eat using one's tortilla to pick up the food, although silverware will be set on the table in the highest income homes. In the other homes, not using silverware indicates that the person is one of the group; my acceptance as a member of the family in the home where I lived was indicated when silverware was no longer set out for me at mealtimes. This pattern is also found in lower income urban households. However, eating with a tortilla in upper-middle class urban homes is severely frowned on. It is permissible, however, to place food on one's tortilla – providing that it is done with a fork.

Foods used for holidays are usually also of high prestige value. Christmas foods for lower household income Arroyo Lindo and migrant households were usually some combination of *tamales*, *bunuelos* (deep fried flour tortilla dough), *menudo*, *barbacoa*, enchiladas and *posole*, while most of those born in the city just ate *tamales*. Turkey, sometimes also served with *tamales* (and/or *bunuelos*, *menudo*, etc. – the "holiday combination") was the most popular Christmas food at higher household incomes. Lower household income households also use the "holiday combination" on New Year's, as do higher household income households in Arroyo Lindo and among the migrants. The "holiday combination" is popular at New Year's among those born in the city, as is the use of turkey or other roasted meat, such as pork or ham.

During Lent, no meat is eaten on Fridays, and there is a variety of special foods that are used in place of the meat, including: fish; seafood; cheese dishes such as squash and cheese (*calavasitas*); cheese and potato soup (*caldo de queso*); or cheese enchiladas; omelette or green beans with red chile sauce (*torta de huevo*, or *ejotes con chile*); greens (*quelites*); and hominy in soup (*chicos*). A Lenten dessert is *capirotada*, a bread pudding made with molasses, regional cheese, and dried fruits. A household of greater means, such as that of Olivia, ate shrimp instead of a meat dish, while a poorer household, such as that of Patricia, would substitute *chicos* for a *caldo*. *Quelites* are of very low prestige under normal circumstances, as they are associated with the poor. Eating *quelites*, which can be gathered wild (although they are usually purchased these days), indicates that you are unable to afford something better. One woman in Arroyo Lindo, with whom I was eating *quelites* one day expressed surprise that I was willing to eat such food. She volunteered that she had not admitted eating *quelites* to those who had conducted the recent nutrition study in Arroyo Lindo. But consumption of *quelites* becomes slightly more acceptable during Lent.

In Arroyo Lindo households of lower household incomes, Lenten foods are either the cheese, eggs, or chile dishes, or fish. The migrants and those born in the city add use of shrimp and other seafood. Rural and migrant households of higher household incomes use similar foods during Lent, although 18–20% drop the use of the cheese, egg, or chile dishes entirely. Those born in the city are even more likely to drop use of the traditional Lenten cheese, egg, or chile dishes. Lenten foods are also used during Holy Week (Semana Santa), either Wednesday through Friday, or Thursday and Friday by the rural and migrant households of lower household incomes. Those born in the city tend to use the Lenten foods for fewer days during Semana Santa. Arroyo Lindo households of higher household incomes use Lenten foods all week, while the migrants use them only Thursday and Friday, and those born in the city use them only on Friday of Holy Week. It would seem that the importance of Semana Santa is greater in the rural areas, and that increased income leads to greater use of special holiday foods only for rural households of higher household incomes. The urban household of the same economic level moves in the opposite direction – perhaps because Holy Week is more obvious as a special period in the rural areas, where there are processions on Thursday and Friday.

Other occasions on which prestige foods are commonly used include visits from friends or relatives, and family celebrations. At the smaller scale family celebrations, such as baptisms, chicken salad, saltines, macaroni salad (*sopa fria*), and cake are commonly used. For weddings, households of lower household incomes use *barbacoa* – meat that is put in a metal drum with other ingredients and then buried in an ash lined pit to cook. A fairly standard recipe is:

1 cow – 2–3 years old
1 young goat
2 kg. garlic – peeled
2 kg. potatoes – chopped
4 small jars green olives
7 small cans tomato puree
4 small cans pickled jalapeno chiles
8 pkg. black pepper (1 pkg approximately = 1 1/2 tbsp)
6 pkg. bay leaves
4 pkg. oregano
3 kg. onions – chopped
1 six pack Tecate brand beer
salt

Grease the drum with 1/2 kg. vegetable shortening. Layer the meat and the other ingredients (it is not necessary to take the meat off the bones). Cover with clean cloths. Cook in a pit of hot ashes for 12 hours, though the meat can be left buried for as long as 3 to 4 days.

Barbacoa, which represents well the Sonoran concept of relative food values (lots of meat, with only token vegetables allowed) is served on unfried corn tortillas with a bit of shredded cabbage and a mild *salsa*. These tacos are accompanied with beans and cheese. The extensive use of shortening in "beans and cheese" is also indicative of the local value system. A standard recipe for beans and cheese is:

Mix:
1 kg. cooked and blended pinto beans
1/2 kg. vegetable shortening
2 sticks of margarine
2 pkg. red chile
1 small can evaporated milk
1 can pickled jalapeno chiles – blended
1/2 kg. of regional cheese (or half regional cheese and half American cheese (queso amarillo))

Higher income rural and migrant households also serve *barbacoa* at weddings. Those born in the city serve barbacoa, or roasted ham or turkey.

House guests will usually be offered daily food or a meat dish by households of lower household incomes. Households of higher household incomes follow a similar pattern, with the exception of those born in the city who serve either regular food or a high prestige meat dish such as *carne asada* (steak), roast pork, or chop suey. For a dinner party (*cena*), rural households of lower household incomes will serve foods from the "holiday combination," while the migrants and those born in the city use chicken salad or *barbacoa*. Arroyo Lindo households of higher household incomes serve a variety of *barbacoa*, "holiday combination" foods, meat dishes, and chicken salad, while the migrants favor *barbacoa*. Those born in the city, however, serve grilled steak (*carne asada*) or chicken, or roasted pork or other meat. Thus, the migrants of higher household incomes tend to use rural rather than urban prestige foods. The latter tend to be either grilled or roasted.

Individual likes and dislikes of foods seem to largely follow prestige lines, with the exception of eggs, which are the food most frequently disliked by the wives. Husbands have few dislikes, with the exception of those born in the city of the highest household incomes who prefer beef served by itself to any kind of mixed up dish, or non-beef meats, or fish. Children of lower household incomes most frequently dislike *caldos*, *sopas*, vegetables, and some meat dishes. (Note that many of these are extremely common foods eaten in these households.) Angelica noted that her older children don't like *caldos*, to the extent that they refuse to eat them. Rural children of higher household incomes tend to dislike some meats and some dairy products, while migrant children of higher household incomes dislike *caldos* and *sopas*. Urban born children of higher household incomes have the most dislikes, and prefer to have as little as possible to do with vegetables, *caldos*, *sopas*, and *atoles* (corn based hot drinks). Other than eggs, dislikes of wives' of lower household incomes include beans, *sopas*, and *caldos*, with urban born women having the most dislikes. This pattern continues at the higher household incomes, where the urban born wives tend to dislike vegetables. The vegetables most disliked by all household members are those of low prestige: squash, *quelites*, and cabbage; even children will usually tolerate lettuce and tomato on a sub sandwich (*torta*) or hamburger.

What is striking about these likes and dislikes is not only the extent to which dislikes follow prestige lines, but also the extent to which people of lower household incomes dislike their own daily foods. This pattern may be why it is so often found that the poor will use additional income not to increase their food supply but to upgrade the quality of their diets. Further, while *caldos* and *sopas* are the most universally disliked foods, they may be continued to be made at least in part because of their low cost. Moreover, care of teeth tends to be neglected at lower household incomes, and many adults are missing teeth. Therefore, soft wet foods, such a *caldos* and *sopas* will be easier to eat than drier harder ones.

A final indication of prestige is the foods that friends, neighbors, and relatives exchange. Main dishes, and foods from holidays and/or celebrations are those most commonly exchanged. However, it is only among those born in the city of the highest household incomes that homemade flour tortillas assume such high prestige value; in this income group, flour tortillas are usually purchased, as only lower household income women make them daily. These tortillas are given to friends, relatives, and neighbors on those rare occasions when they are made.

Prestige – Summary

Prestige is a very important aspect of foods commonly used in Sonora. Meat and other protein foods are associated with the rich; beans and tortillas are associated with the poor. Individual likes and dislikes largely follow prestige lines, with lower income people expressing dislike for many of the foods which comprise their daily diet.

ETHNICITY

This section will focus on: the importance of traditional food beliefs in affecting food consumption patterns; how different ethnic groups view the

foods typical of other groups; when income is controlled, whether households of different ethnic backgrounds eat differently; and, in what ways
food habits most sharply differ by ethnic groups.

While there may indeed be a "hot" and "cold" classification of foods in
Sonora, questions as to what were defined as *comidas frias, comidas frescas*
and *comidas calientes* brought responses of salads and other refrigerated
foods as being cold and cooked foods as being hot. It appeared initially that,
as Clark (1959) had suggested, the traditional categories of "hot" and "cold"
had been reclassified in terms of temperatures of the foods. However,
numerous chance comments made to me, as well as my observations, indicate that there is some sort of more traditional hot–cold classification system
operative. Women who had been ironing or making tortillas, and therefore
had "hot" hands, usually waited until their hands "cooled" before beginning
any other task. I observed that fresh regional cheese was considered to be
"muy fresca" (very cool), and was therefore not eaten by those who had a
cold. Nor were cold things, such as cold meat touched, or anything cold
drunk under those circumstances. When a friend had several teeth pulled,
she told me that she needed to avoid beans, cheese, chile, and pork for several days, as they were "muy frescas." A teen-aged girl in an upper income
urban household was making some fresh orange juice when her mother and
I came in. Her mother told her it would be better for her to drink some tea,
as she was menstruating and orange juice was "muy fresca."

Despite these occurrences, the food beliefs that are most conscious in
this population are those of the "dieta," or the special diet for nursing
women. For forty days after childbirth, no beans, pork, or chile should be
eaten, as they make the uterus cold. However, beer can be drunk as it
increases the amount of milk produced. Other acceptable foods include
atoles, toasted tortillas, chicken, milk, oatmeal, *sopas, caldos,* and *cafe
con leche.* Bathing is prohibited, as is cutting the child's fingernails or toe-
nails, as doing so will adversely affect the child's vision; the child wears
gloves to avoid scratching itself.

The mere presence of a food belief is no indication of how widely and
by whom it is observed. Few households of lower household incomes
mentioned foods to avoid in pregnancy, and those that did so encouraged
avoidance of chile, greasy food, acid foods, soda, pork, and fish.
Households of higher household incomes, particularly among the migrants
and those born in the city noted more foods to be avoided: the migrants
stressed avoiding chile, while those born in the city counseled against eating fattening foods as well. Those in Arroyo Lindo thought it most important to avoid spicy and acid food, as well as pork and fish.

Rural and urban born households of all household incomes advised
nursing women to eat oatmeal, *sopas, atoles,* milk, *caldos,* beer, and soft

boiled eggs. The migrants agreed and felt that chicken, toasted tortillas, dried beef (*carne machaca*), and bread and butter should be included in the diet. Rural households of lower household incomes felt that nursing women should avoid beans, chile, cabbage, grease, citrus fruits, soda, eggs, cheese, pork, fish, and alcohol. The migrants said that pork and fish could be safely eaten if the other foods were avoided. Those born in the city felt that the migrant diet, plus alcohol, was acceptable for the nursing woman. The patterns of households of higher household incomes were similar. Those who had followed the "dieta" themselves were predominantly among the migrants, though the majority of migrants did not observe the "dieta."

While a conscious hot–cold classification was hard to elicit in Sonora, the food avoidances for pregnancy and lactation largely involve foods that are elsewhere in Mexico often considered to be "cold" (Graedon 1976; Lewis 1951). Further, the foods to avoid in pregnancy and while lactating are generally low prestige foods in Sonora – pork, fish, beans, cabbage, eggs. (Pork has higher prestige than beef only for those born in the city of the very highest income group, and even then only in terms of holiday usage.) Foods that are recommended for nursing women tend to be high prestige foods – chicken, beef, bread (similar to Wonder Bread) and butter, milk, and beer.

The prestige values of both the avoided and recommended foods suggest that a detrimental nutritional impact due to following these food beliefs is not to be expected; this outcome also seems even more unlikely when the characteristics of those who hold such beliefs are examined. Based on their responses to the questions on food beliefs related to pregnancy and lactation, each household was classified as either traditional or modern. Those with traditional food beliefs regarding pregnancy had higher household incomes, and tended to live in Arroyo Lindo. No significant differences were noted in household incomes of those who had traditional food beliefs regarding lactation, nor were there significant differences by sample group of those who held and those who did not hold such beliefs. Many of those who held traditional food beliefs themselves felt that the beliefs were old-fashioned and more typical of the rural areas. However, we can conclude that the people who hold these beliefs, be they old-fashioned or not, can largely afford to do so, and that the nutritional impact of such beliefs is likely to be insignificant.

Another common food belief in Sonora concerns the beverages it is advisable to drink when one comes indoors after being out in the sun. At lower household incomes, 65% of the total sample advised avoidance of cold drinks in favor of room temperature water or hot coffee. At higher household incomes, 62% concurred, although this figure was higher in the rural and urban born households (80%, 70%) than among the migrants (46%).

The most fascinating of Sonoran food beliefs concerns foods that should not be eaten together, usually watermelon and milk. At lower household incomes, the belief that watermelon and milk eaten together caused vomiting, headache, congestion, poisoning, intoxication, and/or diarrhea was least common among the low income migrants. At higher household incomes, those of Arroyo Lindo tended to have a greater faith in this belief. However, in addition to the belief that watermelon and milk is a bad combination, there exist many similar beliefs, some involving sardines, the word for which in Spanish (*sardinas*) is similar to "sandia" (watermelon). The total list of bad combinations that seem to be derived from that of watermelon and milk includes: sardines and milk, shrimp and milk; seafood and watermelon; watermelon and beer; saguaro fruit and milk; medicines and sardines; seafood and pork; fish and milk; sardines and watermelon; pork and milk; watermelon and alcohol; watermelon and cantaloupe; tuna and milk; pork and watermelon; watermelon and banana; fish and watermelon; fish, watermelon, and milk; milk and beans; and milk and cucumbers. The only pattern that this list brings to mind is that of Lewis (1951), who reports that fish, milk, and watermelon are all considered to be cold foods.

The belief that combining watermelon and milk is bad is quite firmly held, even in the face of evidence to the contrary. I visited two shops in downtown Hermosillo where fruit and milk drinks (*licuados*) were sold. In the first store, which had on its menu a watermelon and milk *licuado*, the young women behind the counter told me that they sold them, but not as frequently as other kinds of *licuados*. She had, however, heard that *licuados* of watermelon and milk could kill you, had never tried one, and had no intention of doing so. In the next store, a middle-aged man told me that watermelon and milk *licuados* don't cause any harm, but that because watermelon has so much water in it, you really don't need to add any milk. He, however, does not make watermelon and milk *licuados*.

Another aspect of ethnic food traditions is the issue of how different ethnic groups view the foods typical of other groups. At lower household incomes, American food tended to be defined in terms of stereotypes – hamburgers, hot dogs, fried chicken, sandwiches – although the migrants focused on foods commonly bought in the United States, as well as vegetable salads. Some of those born in the city also included in their definition of American food such items as pizza, spaghetti, and chop suey. At higher household incomes, those in Arroyo Lindo focused on either the stereotypes or canned foods; the migrants mentioned the stereotypes and foods usually bought in the United States; those born in the city considered the stereotypes as well as pizza, etc. to be American. Most considered these foods to be American because they were either used there or they had eaten them on visits to the United States. For example, Sandra felt that hamburgers, french fries and ketchup, ice cream, and grilled cheese sandwiches were American as this is what her daughter ordered when she and her mother had eaten in restaurants in Los Angeles. A frequently mentioned aspect disliked about American food was that it was too bland and lacking in spices, especially salt.

In contrast, the Americans tended to define American food as either fast food or foods usually eaten when just the family was present. The latter category includes foods such as beef stew, steak and potatoes, the meat-vegetable starch meal format, potato salad, corn on the cob, bacon and eggs for breakfast, pot roast, baked pork chops, roast beef, strawberry shortcake, casseroles (especially tuna casserole), fried chicken, barbecued spareribs, baked chicken, veal and lamb chops, and the most frequently mentioned dish – meat loaf. These foods were considered to be American predominantly because they were used in the United States, although some stressed that they were not available or not made well in Mexico. Aspects disliked about American food were its reliance on chemicals, artificial ingredients, and junk and prepared food. Several also complained that they found American food too bland.

It is interesting to note the extent to which the Americans stereotyped American food. In comparison with the types of foods consumed in the United States in the early 1980's, their list of American foods is very narrow, and represents a kind of Midwestern, middle American image. No "ethnic foods" are included on the list, in spite of the widespread use of such foods in the United States at that time.

At lower household incomes, Mexican definitions of Mexican food included stereotypes (such as fried tacos and *tostadas*), many of the foods of the "holiday combination," as well as some daily foods such as beans, tortillas, potatoes, and *caldos*. Arroyo Lindo and those born in the city in particular mentioned the daily foods; the migrants also focused on typical Sonoran foods (such as *caldo de queso*, *carne asada*, green corn tamales, and *carne machaca*), and *mole* and *chilaquiles* – foods more typical of central and southern Mexico. At higher household incomes, Arroyo Lindo and those born in the city listed the stereotypes, the "holiday combination," and home foods; the migrants focused on Sonoran and southern foods. My favorite of all of the Mexican definitions of Mexican food was that of Isabel, who considered Mexican food to be "beans and coffee, because they are never lacking in any Mexican house." Generally Mexican foods were so considered because they are eaten in Mexico. Aspects frequently disliked were most commonly expressed by those born in the city, and were that the food was too spicy; those born in the city of higher incomes found it too greasy as well.

The Americans tended to define Mexican food according to pre-immigrant stereotypes of Mexican food, as seen in items such as *tostadas* and fried tacos, which are served in the U.S. as "Mexican food." In Mexico the taco is usually made with an unfried tortilla. Also considered Mexican were the "holiday combination foods" and daily foods, although some added foods of southern Mexico. These respondents felt that "real" Mexican food consisted of the typical dishes used in the central and southern part of the country; Sonoran dishes such as *carne asada* would not be considered "typical" Mexican food.

Others focused on the ways in which Mexican food contrasts with American food – they saw the former as being more time consuming to fix as well as being served differently, i.e., in different courses (*sopa*, main dish, etc.), as opposed to the American style of serving all of the foods on one plate (meat, starch, vegetable). Betty objected to Mexican foods and Mexican serving patterns in that they depended on the wife spending most of the meal standing at the stove – serving courses, heating tortillas, etc. The Americans felt that the foods they considered to be Mexican were so defined because of their ingredients (corn and chile), as well as because they are fried. The main complaint was that Mexican food was too greasy and fattening, although several also objected to the use of variety meats. Ellen specified, "*menudo*, pigs' feet, intestines, head – it makes me nauseous just to think about them."

An interesting aspect of these results is that the Americans tended to consider American food to be the kinds of foods eaten on a daily basis, while the Mexicans often define Mexican foods as those of the "holiday combination." The foods considered by the Americans to be American tended to be either baked and/or American style one-pot meals. Thus, the Americans have defined as American foods those dishes that contrast most greatly with Mexican style cooking, which has different one-pot meals, and which rarely uses the oven. This pattern may reflect the situation of the Americans living in a foreign country; it would be most interesting to compare this pattern with that of Americans living in the United States.

When income is controlled, there are few differences in basic food consumption between the Americans and urban-born Mexicans. Even when just the households of Americans married to Americans are compared with those of urban born Mexicans, very few significant differences appear (Table 24). However, one difference that these tables do not indicate is in consumption of peanut butter. During the three days for which food consumption was recorded, one third of the American households used peanut butter at least once. The only use of peanut butter by Mexicans was in a

Table 24. Food Consumption of Americans Married to Americans and High Income Urban Born Mexicans – Mean Daily Per Capita Servings

Food type	Americans N = 25 individuals Mean	Mexicans N = 64 individuals Mean	t	p*
Fruit	0.9	1.1	−0.53	n.s.
Veg	0.9	1.2	−1.60	n.s.
Beans	0.2	0.5	−3.52	<0.01
Dairy	2.0	1.9	0.27	n.s.
Eggs	0.7	0.8	−0.78	n.s.
Grains	5.5	4.2	2.88	<0.01
Misc	0.4	0.7	−1.84	n.s.
Pot	0.4	0.2	3.11	<0.01
Meats	1.5	2.0	−1.89	n.s.
Alc	0.0	0.1	−1.50	n.s.

*two-tailed (pooled variance).
Serving Units: Fruit – 1/2 c juice or cooked/canned or 1 medium piece; Vegetable – 1/2 c juice or cooked/canned or 3/4 c raw; Beans – 1/2 c cooked; Dairy – 1 c milk or 1 c plain yogurt or 1 1/3 oz. aged cheese; Eggs – 1 medium egg; Grains – 1 slice bread or 3/4 c cooked cereal, spaghetti, noodles; Misc – 1 soft drink (473 ml) or 1 small package potato chips, etc. or 1 medium sized candy bar or 1 c Kool-Aid; Potato – 1 medium; Meat – 2 to 3 oz. cooked meat or fish; Alcohol – 1 can beer or 1 mixed drink or 1/2 c wine.

high income urban-born household, whose jar of Jiffy had been a gift from American friends. It is interesting that in spite of this high association of the use of peanut butter with households with American wives, there was no mention by them of peanut butter as "American food." Peanut butter, perhaps because it is viewed as a children's food, or due to its non-meat nature, may have a relatively low prestige value. In that food used as, or considered to be ethnic symbols also are of high prestige value, this may explain the omission of peanut butter on lists given by the Americans of "American foods."

The meal patterns of the two groups also differ. Breakfast for the Americans is lighter, and the Mexicans have a greater tendency to use meat at breakfast. American lunches are less likely to include beans and more likely to include vegetables. Fifteen percent of the Americans eat a lunch of the non-Mexican, meat-vegetable-starch format. The Americans eat a heavier evening meal, and are more likely to use meat at that meal. The main starches used by the Americans are rice, potatoes, and bread, while the Mexicans use tortillas, potatoes, and bread. Meat is either fried, baked, or broiled by the Americans, while Mexicans do no baking or broiling, and usually boil then fry, or just fry their meat. Both groups either boil starches or make them as *sopas*. Americans are likely to boil, steam or use vegetables raw, while Mexicans do more boiling and less steaming. Americans are more likely to see time as the most important factor affecting their food consumption patterns, while the Mexicans feel that taste is of prime importance. This pattern may be related to the increased rates of economic activity among the American wives.

Other aspects of food habits also show differences between the ethnic groups. Americans are more likely to use baked meat at Christmas and New Year's, while the Mexicans occasionally use the "holiday combination" foods as well. Few Americans observe Lent or Holy Week. For those who observe Easter Sunday, a non-Mexican holiday, typically American foods such as baked ham, turkey, or fried chicken are used. Thanksgiving, another non-Mexican holiday, is observed by the majority of Americans, who serve turkey with American style trimmings. The persistence of a fixed Thanksgiving menu is very strong; Claire, who considered herself American even though she had never lived in the United States (she was born in Mexico of American parents), served a Thanksgiving dinner of turkey, bread stuffing, mashed potatoes, green vegetables, cranberry sauce, gravy, biscuits, and apple and pumpkin pies; most of these foods were only obtainable via a shopping trip to Tucson. There is some variance in holiday patterns within the American group; the Mexican American women tend to use a Mexican type meat, vegetable, and dried fruit stuffing, while the rest of the Americans used either a homemade or packaged bread based stuffing. In addition, as side dishes for holiday meals, the Mexican Americans often used a *sopa fria*.

We see then, a pattern of use of American foods on holiday occasions. Even the Mexican American women's use of "Mexican" trimmings reflects more their Mexican-American heritage than it does "borrowing" from their Sonoran neighbors. This pattern of use of American foods on holidays may be due to the fact that the Americans are more likely than the Mexicans to have sentimental feelings about holiday foods (especially as they are far from "home"), and increase their use of these foods because of the associations with them.

Other points of difference between the Americans and Mexicans include foods served to house guests and at dinner parties. The Americans make either regular food or American food, international food, or American style Mexican foods (such as meat loaf, prime rib, steak, hamburgers, tacos made with ground beef, fondue, spaghetti, or Chinese food). The Mexicans serve regular food or high prestige Mexican foods (such as *carne asada*, roast pork, or chop suey). The Americans married to Americans are the only Americans who tend to serve "Mexican foods" on these occasions.

Clearly then, the Americans consider American foods to be more appropriate for prestige occasions than Mexican foods. Only the Americans married to Americans break somewhat from the pattern of use of American food on prestige occasions. This may relate to the greater satisfaction this group feels with their lives, or it may reflect a sense of the romance of the exotic. For the rest, use of distinctly American foods on prestige occasions is a way to publicly demonstrate their identity, which is daily questioned by their living situations. The contradictions felt by the Americans married to Mexicans may, paradoxically, be most strong among the Mexican-American women. It is they who tended (before the devaluation) to make regular trips to the United States to do their food shopping. The Mexican environment may actually make these women more aware of the American aspects of their backgrounds. Olivia told me that "the longer I live in Mexico, the more American I feel." Frequent trips to the United States and cupboards full of American groceries may become a kind of symbol for these women, a way of demonstrating their Americanness.

Also different in the Mexican and American groups is the effect on dietary intakes of an economically active wife; few differences in food consumption are seen among the Americans, while for the Mexicans, an economically active wife is associated with decreased fruit, MISC, and meat consumption, and increased dairy consumption. This pattern may be due to the greater dependence of the American women on time saving canned foods and mixes; the Mexicans use more fresh food. Seasonal changes in food consumption are most strongly noted for the Americans, who tend to use more cold food in the summer. This is a non-Mexican pattern; on days where the temperature was over 100 degrees F, it was not at all unusual to be served a hot bowl of soup at lunch in a Mexican household. Baked casseroles are only used by the Americans, although many find that their Mexican husbands and children dislike these dishes.

The two other ethnic differences in food habits are ones most likely to contribute to cultural misunderstanding. Both Americans and Mexicans commonly exchange food with friends and neighbors. However, the Americans consider a gift of food appropriate for any occasion. They feel it is a more intimate gift, and is more appreciated due to the time and special effort making it involved. "It's nicer, as you are giving more of yourself. It shows you cared enough to make it. It's an act of love." While Mexicans feel more trust ("confianza") and friendship is involved with those with whom one shares food, they tend to think that food is not appropriate as a gift.

Finally, when eating at someone else's house, the Americans feel that it is expected that you will clean your plate and express your enjoyment by saying so. Mexicans very strongly believe that leaving a small bit of food on the plate is the appropriate manner in which to demonstrate your satisfaction with the meal. They say that unless there is a relationship of extreme trust among the people involved ("son de mucha confinanza"), they feel bad to clean their plates ("le da pena de dejar el plato limpio"). Not only does it look "ugly" to leave your plate empty, but there is the chance that your hosts will think you were "dying of hunger." If in fact you are still hungry, you are advised to hide it.

Ethnicity – Summary

The data reveal a number of interesting ethnic food habits, from food beliefs to behavior at a dinner party. However, when income is controlled, these ethnic food habits have little actual impact on diets. Ethnic food habits, however, may reveal a great deal about how the ethnic group sees itself and others. Also, the food habits of one ethnic group may on occasion, contribute to misunderstandings on the part of those of different ethnic backgrounds.

DESIRES FOR CONSUMER GOODS

The differential importance of ovens to Mexican and American wives has been previously discussed. The reverse pattern is true of blenders, which are used much more by the Mexican wives. Moving beyond these issues, this section examines the order in which selected types of consumer goods are acquired. Also considered is the extent to which desires for consumer goods compete with food as a household expenditure.

One of the major occasions on which consumer goods are acquired is Mothers' Day. In 1982 Pablo bought his mother a television, in the previous year a gas stove. Lucia received a washing machine from her husband on Mothers' Day 1981. A Guttman Scale was constructed of the order in which the sample households acquired selected consumer goods items. From first to last item acquired, the order is: gas stove, electricity, cement floor, refrigerator, blender, television, car or truck, kitchen sink, indoor bathroom, washing machine, and telephone. Note that the items that contribute most toward reduction of women's work – gas stove, refrigerator, blender, kitchen sink, and washing machine, are among the first and last items acquired.

A consumer goods ranking was established by determining how many of the selected consumer goods items a household owned. However, multiple ownership of one item did not affect a household's ranking. There are no significant differences by sample group in consumer goods ranking among lower household income households; at higher household incomes, Arroyo Lindo households have the lowest ranking, while the urban born have the highest. There are no significant differences in consumer goods ranking by household structure, which indicates that the portion of their incomes that other household workers do not contribute to household heads in multiple worker households does not usually come back into the household in the form of appliances, etc. Consumer goods ranking increases as do both household and available incomes.

Food consumption varies significantly by consumer goods ranking for all food groups except MISC and alcohol (Figure 4, 5). The values at several consumer goods rankings decrease unexpectedly for several food types: fruit (rankings 6 to 8), vegetables (rankings 4 to 6), dairy (rankings 5 to 9), and meat (rankings 5 to 7). They increase unexpectedly for other food types: beans (rankings 5 to 8), grains (rankings 5 to 8), and potatoes (rankings 5 to 8). Multiple regression tests were performed to assess non-linear trends in relationships between mean household food consumption of each food type and household consumer goods ranking. Significant ($p < 0.01$) non-linear effects were seen for fruit, vegetables, beans, dairy, MISC, and meat. This pattern suggests that beginning with the attainment of consumer goods ranking 6 (+television) and continuing until after ranking 7 (+car/truck), there may be some decreases in food expenditures to make acquisition of these consumer items possible. It may be at this stage that desires for consumer goods rise beyond a household's ability to

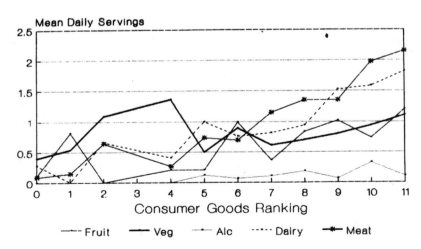

Figure 4. Food Consumption by Consumer Goods Ranking: Fruit, Vegetables, Alcohol, Dairy, and Meat.

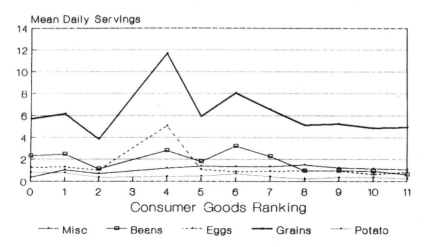

Figure 5. Food Consumption by Consumer Goods Ranking: Miscellaneous, Beans, Eggs, Grains, and Potatoes.

acquire them without substitution of less expensive foods (such as beans) for more expensive ones (fruit, vegetables, dairy, MISC, and meat). It is clear that households, even at relatively low income levels are willing to make trade-offs between quality of diet and ownership of certain types of consumer goods. This may be particularly true given the nature of the consumer items of rankings 6 and 7 (televisions and vehicles).

These kinds of dietary quality versus consumer goods trade-offs are those of which the "envidious" generally accused their neighbors. Thus, the conclusions regarding "envidia" suggested in the prestige section may need to be expanded. Envidious comments may actually be made by those among the upwardly mobile who have rejected the trade-offs of diet for more consumer goods which they see many of their neighbors making. Their comments, which have been interpreted as reflecting envy, may really represent reality, and may therefore be designed to indicate the true lack of difference between their households and those of their neighbors. The latter may have achieved their public appearance of greater means only by making reductions in the quality of their diets.

Desires for Consumer Goods – Summary

Consumer goods that reduce women's work are among the first and last items acquired. Household appear to be willing to make trade-offs between dietary quality and consumer goods acquisition, especially if the item involved is a television or car/truck. The pattern is one of substitution of less expensive foods for more expensive ones.

NUTRITIONAL KNOWLEDGE

The high levels of consumption of MISC, and extent of nutritional problems suggests that the nutritional knowledge of the sample populations may be inadequate. This section considers the extent to which nutritional knowledge of the wife correlates with place of residence or income level. Also discussed is the extent to which increased nutritional knowledge on the part of the wife affects patterns of food consumption.

At higher household income levels, most households saw a relationship between foods consumed and state of health, although this perception was lowest among the migrants. At lower household incomes, only 33% of the wives thought there was a relationship between food and health. Among those who did not perceive such a relationship, their comments included, "Some people eat well but are very thin; some eat poorly but are fat," and "my kids don't eat that well, but they're not sick. It depends on what you're used to – someone used to better food might not do well on what my children eat." The latter comment was made by a migrant wife, many of whose children were very small for their age. This situation, however, is not perceived as unusual. As I was weighing and measuring children in Arroyo Lindo, the mothers tended to express concern about the health of children who were second degree malnourished; the stunting characteristic of most of the first degree malnourished children went unnoticed.

To what extent does this apparent lack of nutritional knowledge of the wives affect actual dietary intakes? On the basis of each wife's answers to the questions on food and health, and important foods to eat for good health, the households were ranked on their level of nutritional knowledge: none – "no relationship between what you eat and your state of health"; least – "if you're sick eat special foods" or "some foods can make you sick"; less – "yes, there's a relationship between food and health. Eat varied foods" (including protein foods); most – "yes, there's a relationship between food and health. Eat varied foods" (including use of vegetables and/or foods with vitamins). "Most" and "less" were differentiated because the typical Sonoran is more likely to omit vegetables from the diet than protein foods. Greater nutritional knowledge tends to be associated with higher household income (Table 25). Julia, one of the poorest women in the sample, was very clear that important foods to eat were vegetables, fruit, and red and white meats, but she also added that "we can't afford to eat those things."

Table 25. Per Capita Household Income Level and Nutrition Knowledge Ranking

Income Level	Nutritional Knowledge Ranking*			
	Most	*Less*	*Least*	*None*
Lower Income N* = 44 HH	10	9	4	21
Higher income N* = 34 HH	18	5	5	6
Chi Square 11.06771				
p 0.0114				

see text: N – Weighted N; HH = Households.

Another indication of the relative lack of importance of nutritional knowledge in producing different nutritional outcomes is seen by reviewing the findings of the comparative study of Arroyo Lindo, Milpas Verdes, and Los Cerritos. While it is possible (though not very likely, given the degree of social interaction) that there are significantly different levels of nutritional knowledge among the three villages, the data suggest that the most important factor influencing nutritional status in those villages is differential access to land and water, and resulting differences in home production and available income.

Nutritional Knowledge – Summary

Lower income households were less likely to see a relationship between food and health, and greater nutritional knowledge was associated with being of higher income. Nevertheless, other factors appear to be of much greater importance in affecting food consumption patterns than is amount of nutritional knowledge.

CONCLUSIONS

The results of the analyses of this chapter and Chapter 3 point to available income as being a key factor affecting food consumption patterns. The variables discussed in this chapter are critical in the way they affect allocation of available income. Prestige loadings of goods often seem to discourage use of nutritionally valuable foods, and desires for consumer goods may cause a decrease in dietary quality, though not among households of the very lowest incomes. While ethnic food patterns are not shown to be an important factor in this study, they may be so where groups who are not elites are involved. Finally, the data presented here suggest that the social and cultural variables of least importance in affecting Sonoran food consumption patterns are traditional food beliefs and nutritional knowledge.

CHAPTER 5

Out of the Frying Pan...and into the Fire
Conclusions

On the basis of the Sonoran study, as well as the literature in general, this chapter will make general conclusions as to the role of the social and

cultural variables that have been under consideration here. These conclusions will be applied to an understanding of the causality of the types of
nutritional problems observed in rural and urban Sonora, Mexico. Recommendations will be made as to how the variables could be manipulated to
improve nutritional outcomes. Finally, these recommendations will be
considered in the light of the direction Mexico has moved since the
mid-1980's.

THE EFFECTS OF SOCIAL AND CULTURAL VARIABLES

Available Income

One of the more significant differences between the patterns of the
Sonoran data and those of the literature is that the former posit a clear relationship among the social and cultural variables under consideration here.
While the literature suggests an unclear pattern of interactions, this study
illustrates the way in which this interaction is related to the "invisible variable" of available income. The other variables either affect amount of
available income or how this amount is allocated. In that the concept of
available income incorporates the effects of several other variables, it
would be a highly useful tool to use to analyze relationships between
income and nutritional status.

This is particularly true in areas of the world where households are likely
to be of the multiple worker type (unlike the prevailing situation in the
United States). It is likely that the non-correlations between income and
nutritional status in many locales might disappear if per capita available
income were used in analyses, instead of total household per capita income.
The focus of study then becomes one of understanding the household level
behaviors and situations which cause similar amounts of total household
income to result in different amounts of available income. This analysis
must be supplemented by investigation into the factors that influence how
available income will be spent.

In the Sonoran case, available income was computed in terms of mean
per capita household available income. In fact, due to allocation patterns,
some household members have greater amounts of income available to
them than do others. For example, a working child who contributes part of
his/her earnings to his/her parents, has also available to him/her the rest
of that income to spend on his/her own food or any other personal expenditures. In general, males tend to have greater amounts of income available for meeting their individual wants (females tend to not to retain as
much money for "personal" expenses) (Whitehead 1981), but the approach
to available income taken here was not based on general differences in the

way men versus women spend their earnings. This type of focus is seen somewhat in the literature (Dwyer 1983), but tends to imply that gender-based differences in income allocation patterns are the most important. Since there is general agreement in Sonora that it is the husband's responsibility to provide money to cover basic household expenses, I have focused instead on the importance of the person's role in the household, and the effects of this factor on how that person's income is allocated. Women may tend to spend more of their earnings on household expenses, but in Sonora, the critical difference in income allocation is not based on gender but generation – i.e., the ways in which parents and children allocate their earnings is more different than the male/female distinction.

This type of differentiation of role from gender in consideration of available income may be important in other situations as well. Whitehead's (1981) data from northeastern Ghana suggested that men, women, and children over the age of 10 all have some form of cash income over which they have complete control. Further, two-thirds of the households consist of between five and twenty adults.

The concept of available income thus challenges the assumptions that underlie much of contemporary food policy. Many of those involved in food policy analysis have not addressed the issue of household income allocation patterns (Timmer, Falcon and Pearson 1983; Gittinger et al., 1987). Other contemporary theorists have assumed that households pool all of their income resources (Becker 1981). This model of household behavior, termed "the New Home Economics," attempts to explain micro-level household behavior, and has been applied to households around the world. One critique of this approach has been in terms of the behavior of husbands and wives, who, in areas such as west Africa, do not pool their incomes (Fapohunda 1988). Yet prior to the study described in this book, no attention had been given to the issue of multiple worker households, and to the effects that allocation patterns in these households have on income availability. Given the frequency with which households of this type appear in the developing world, it is no wonder that many projects designed to alleviate food and nutritional problems at the household level have failed.

OTHER VARIABLES

Rural to Urban Migration

The Sonora data confirm the patterns suggested in the literature (Kemper 1981; Roberts 1973; Herrick 1965; Simmons and Cardona 1972; Bradfield 1973; Carvajal and Geithman 1974; Butterworth 1962; Chavez et al.,

1976; Immink *et al.*, 1983; Graedon 1976; Black and Sanjur 1980); rural to urban migrants tend to be positively selected by household income, educational levels, and dietary patterns with regard to both place of origin (Arroyo Lindo) and place of destination (Hermosillo). While the food consumption patterns of the migrants do not consistently follow those of either the rural or urban born households, migrants of lower household incomes have retained a number of nutritionally positive rural food consumption patterns that may reduce their nutritional risk. In addition, the persistence of the rural tradition of economic activity of women is seen in the Arroyo Lindo migrants. Both of these aspects of migrant behavior raise the available incomes of their households. However, these largely positive effects of rural to urban migration are only confirmed for situations in which a transition from a subsistence economy to one of wage labor is not made, and in which there are few changes in availability or costs of foods.

The effects of rural to urban migration on the rural areas suggested in the literature (Preston 1969; Bradfield 1973; Perlman 1976; Chavez *et al.*, 1976; Shadow 1979; Morrison 1977) are also confirmed by the Sonoran data. Simply due to the demographic effects of nutritionally positively selective out-migration, nutritional problems increase in the rural areas. Further, the loss to the rural community of its more educated members creates a situation where economic problems, a causal factor of migration (and which are often responsible for nutritional problems), become a consequence of it as well. The result is the creation of a downwardly spiraling cycle that becomes very difficult to break, especially in the absence of governmental attention toward the underlying causes of economic problems in the rural areas.

Income and Women's Roles

Both the literature (Berg 1973; Au Coin *et al.*, 1972; Greiner and Latham 1981; Dewalt and Pelto 1976; Dewalt *et al.*, 1980) and the Sonoran data show a clear link between income and dietary intake. However, issues of allocation of different types of income prove to be key. The patterns of women's income being likely to positively effect food consumption reported by Tripp (1982), Guyer (1980) and Kumar (1978), and being directed towards household versus personal expenses (Whitehead 1981; Salaff 1981) are also seen in Sonora. This finding is important in that women's power is probably less in the ranching world of Sonora than in the African matrilineal areas studied by Guyer (1980) and Tripp (1982). Thus, the finding of this pattern in Sonora indicates that it may be found around the world.

Wives' work patterns at the higher income levels follow those of Arizpe (1977) i.e., work is done predominantly part-time and at home, and thus there is little conflict with adequate childcare. Lower household income wives also tend toward part-time work in the informal sector, which enables them to devote adequate care to their children as well. Thus, the role of the informal sector, generally considered not to contribute to over-all productivity, may need to be re-evaluated, as in many cases, it serves to transfer money into the hands of women.

Working and economically active wives also devote adequate time to other of their "traditional" roles, such as cooking. In addition, working and economically active wives may be better able to cope with financial emer-gencies without being forced to reduce expenditures on food. Wife's work, which tends to be less than full-time (Sonoran patterns and the structure of the study created a bias against the inclusion of wives who worked full-time in the sample), positively affects household food consumption because it causes few conflicts with childcare, and increases available income because of the way in which it is spent. Income earned by other household members does not have a great affect on the amount of income available for household expenses, including the purchasing of food, although it may raise the individual available incomes of the other wage earners.

Intra-Household Distribution of Food

Much of the correlation cited in the literature between household size and nutritional problems (Wray and Aguirre 1969) may actually be due to dif-ferences in per capita income among the households. When income is con-trolled, the Sonoran data do not support the contention that poorer diets are more common in larger households due to preferential access to food on the part of older household members (Whiteford 1982). While dietary intakes of most food types are lower in larger households, so also are per capita household and available incomes. This pattern is related to the fre-quency with which larger households are of the multiple worker type, in which available incomes tend to be much lower than in non-multiple worker households.

Subsistence Pattern

As suggested by the literature (Fleuret and Fleuret 1980), some of the nutritional problems in rural Sonora may be due to the shift that has taken place there over the past few decades from subsistence to market produc-tion. Further, the findings of Smith et al. (1983), which show that even small amounts of home production (as from a family garden) can have a significant positive impact on food consumption (because available income is increased), are confirmed not only in terms of the comparison of the rural, migrant, and urban-born households, but also in the comparison of growth of children in Arroyo Lindo, Milpas Verdes, and Los Cerritos.

In addition, the latter comparison, when considered with the data presented by Fleuret and Fleuret (1983), suggests conditions under which commercial agriculture is not associated with increased nutritional risk. First, it appears that continued production for home use is important. Second, in both cases, the communities with greater access to essential economic resources experience improved nutritional status, i.e., Milpas Verdes has access to the irrigation water, while Iparenyl (the village described by Fleuret and Fleuret 1983) has access to outside cash income. These resources are of a nature that allows considerable flexibility for their users to adapt to differing market or other conditions. This resiliency of production strategy (which usually incorporated some elements of commercial agriculture) has been identified as being critical in avoiding the undermining of household nutriture associated with commercial agriculture (Fleuret and Fleuret 1991).

This access to essential resources may also affect the available income of the people in these communities. In the Sonoran example, mean household income may not differ greatly among the three villages. However, the ranchers of Milpas Verdes are likely to have greater available income as they are not spending a large portion of their earnings on food for cattle. There are no income data provided for Iparenyl, but it appears that available income in Iparenyl is greater than in the other farming communities.

The issue is therefore not one of inevitable nutritional effects of cash cropping, but may be related to the circumstances thereof. In the situations discussed above, cash cropping is associated with nutritional benefits only because the farmers/ranchers involved have also had access to the resources – irrigation water or outside cash income – which have enabled them to be successful in commercial agriculture. We need to reassess whether it is cash cropping which is the problem, or rather trying to carry out this subsistence strategy in the absence of the necessary inputs. I strongly suspect that the latter is a common situation. Therefore, our indictment should not be of involvement in commercial agriculture per se, but of its spread without the accompanying access to the necessary economic resources, which unfortunately continues to be the situation in most of the Third World.

Prestige

The literature suggests that prestige is one of the more important variables affecting food consumption patterns (Devadas 1970; Leininger 1970;

Bennett, Smith and Passin 1942; Cussler and de Give 1942; Fitzgerald 1976; Anderson and Anderson 1977; Messer 1976). This association is difficult to test quantitatively, but the findings from this study suggest that some of the food consumption patterns of those born in the city of lower household incomes (i.e., the ways in which available income is allocated) may be motivated by the prestige values of the foods involved. However, foods that are of low prestige for one population (e.g., flour tortillas for those born in the city of lower household incomes) may be of high prestige for those of another group (e.g., those born in the city of the very highest household incomes). Those born in the city seem most aware of the prestige loadings of different foods, and may be most likely to suffer greater nutritional consequences due to their avoidance of many highly nutritious foods. While there appears to be a relationship between foods disliked and foods of low prestige, there also seems to be some cross-cultural similarity in these patterns. Nalbandian *et al.*'s (1981) Americans of the third generation no longer "liked" traditional ethnic soups. Moreover, their lists of preferred and disliked vegetables are very similar to those of Sonorans.

Ethnicity

Perhaps because of the lack of Americans of lower household incomes living in Hermosillo with which to make comparisons, this study suggests fewer differences in dietary intakes due to ethnicity than does the cross-cultural literature. However, food habits and customs do vary considerably by ethnic group, even when household income is controlled. This finding suggests that the role of ethnicity may be more important in other situations than in this study. Also, any kind of programs designed to change food consumption patterns would need to take into account the household level ethnic differences in behavior that, for example, make the effect of economically active wives different among the Americans and Mexicans of similar household incomes. There is a definite pattern in Sonora of the less-secure ethnic group – the Americans (and in some cases, especially the Mexican-Americans) – using food as a symbol of their cultural identity, a pattern that also occurs in Malaysia (Anderson and Anderson 1977). As the American households were all of a high income level, this practice carries no negative nutritional implications. However, to the extent that in other situations this behavior may also be characteristic of households of lower household incomes, use of food as an ethnic identity symbol remains an important issue to investigate.

A lack of impact of traditional ethnic food beliefs is also indicated by the Sonoran data. In essence, the minority of women who hold traditional food beliefs can usually afford to do so. Despite a fascinating range of beliefs, the effect of these on nutritional status (similar to the situation described by Laderman [1983] for rural Malaysia) is therefore likely to be insignificant.

Desires for Consumer Goods

There are frequent references in the literature to the poor preferring consumer goods to calories are frequent in the literature (Gray 1982). This study suggests that this pattern may also exist in Sonora, but is most characteristic of households just above the poorest. This preference also seems frequently to be associated with acquisition of relatively expensive items, such as televisions or vehicles.

Nutritional Knowledge

Neither this study, nor others (Dewalt and Pelto 1976; Dewalt *et al.*, 1980) suggest an important role for differences in wives' nutritional knowledge in affecting food consumption patterns. Further, in Sonora, only the presence of more severe nutritional problems is perceived as a problem. And, as discussed below, practices that indicate apparent lack of nutritional knowledge and concerns – such as the extent to which Arroyo Lindo school age children are rarely seen without a piece of candy or soft drink in their hands – may in fact represent nutritionally positive adaptation.

Summary

The results of the Sonora study largely confirm many of the trends seen in the literature. However, one of the more important findings of this project is the identification of the role and importance of available income in understanding variations in diet at the household level. This study indicates that important directions to pursue in the future are: a further understanding of the factors responsible in those situations where total household income does not equal available income; and the factors which influence the ways in which available income will be spent. More research in this area may clarify many issues regarding relationships between income and nutritional status which to this point have remained unresolved.

FACTORS AFFECTING MALNUTRITION IN SONORA

The patterning of malnutrition in Sonora has several aspects. According to Valencia (1980; 1981) significant levels of mild to moderate malnutrition are found in both economically marginal rural and urban areas, with the problem most serious in the urban areas. Most affected are school-age children, while adults were found to be more overweight than any other group. Finally, females appear to be more affected by nutritional problems than are males. Each of these aspects of the overall nutritional situation and the variables discussed in this study that may affect them will be considered separately.

Factors Affecting Rural Malnutrition

The data indicate at least four significant associations with malnutrition: positively selective out-migration; the shift over the past decades to a market economy, the pattern of Sonoran development which has favored large export-oriented growers on *la costa* de Hermosillo and in the Yaqui and Mayo Valleys, and specific to Arroyo Lindo, the unresolved land problems. In Arroyo Lindo, the land problems and cheese market create an extremely positive pattern of out-migration – it is not the poorest who leave. Rather, it is those for whom this type of rural situation blocks opportunities for local upward mobility and who can afford to migrate. This pattern is likely to continue, as those families that indicated that they would consider leaving Arroyo Lindo represent those who tend to be better off economically on a per capita basis (regardless of their situations with respect to landholding) than those families who told me they probably would not consider leaving. However, even the latter group is sending, and intends to continue to send as many children as possible to Hermosillo for advanced schooling. Therefore, the pattern of positively selective out-migration will persist, in spite of the fact that all of these households have close relatives already living in Hermosillo.

Positively selective rural to urban migration is characteristic of Latin America in general, but it is possible that other areas of the Sierra of Sonora may not create such extreme selective pressure among migrants. Because of its land problems, Arroyo Lindo represents a much more serious case than do the neighboring villages in which there is more land owned by true small owners. The existence in the neighboring villages of land that can be bought and sold freely may allow more opportunities for those who choose to avail themselves. These villages generally have fewer land groups (often just one *ejido*), so there may be less potential for intra-village conflict.

While the extreme problems of Arroyo Lindo may not occur in the neighboring villages with which I have had more contact, they may reappear in other areas of Mexico. Even if Arroyo Lindo were an extreme case in Sonora at the present, the pattern may become more common in the future. For example, villages Alto and Bajo, the other two villages

involved in the land disputes with the Perez family, will soon have
exhausted their opportunities to acquire additional land. They, like Arroyo
Lindo, may become a new Middle American community type – a "closed-
in community" where modern improvements hide the basic and unresolved problem of land tenure. People in those villages who are even able
to own cattle may also become caught in a web of purchased cattle food,
cheese production, very highly selective out-migration and ultimately,
increased nutritional problems.

That adequate nutritional status is possible in the Sierra region of
Sonora is illustrated by the case of Milpas Verdes, which has received the
kind of technical aid (development of water resources, to which there is
equal access) recommended for this entire area. But even without such aid
for the Sierra region, the present situation still produces some benefits:
Hermosillo receives capable workers and cheese, the export of beef provides Mexico with badly needed foreign exchange, and the Perez family is
certainly not suffering. But the results of all of this seem to be the creation
of pockets of socially created poverty, and malnutrition. A few such pockets might be tolerable if they result in greater prosperity for the nation as a
whole. However, the pockets may be growing larger than the garment
itself, and therefore a reevaluation of development goals and policies on
the part of the Mexican government may be appropriate.

Factors Affecting Urban Malnutrition

I turn now to the issue of why rates of malnutrition in the urban areas are
higher than those of the rural regions. This situation at first seems to be a
paradox, in that the migrants appear not to be at much nutritional risk due
to their positive selectivity, as well as to retention at the lower income levels of several nutritionally advantageous rural patterns. While the migrants
from Arroyo Lindo may be somewhat more positively selective then
migrants from other areas of the Sierra, the literature on Latin American
rural to urban migration suggests that they are not atypical.

Several issues are important in understanding factors correlated with the
urban nutritional problems: the decreased home production done by the
low income urban born as compared with those of similar income levels in
the rural areas; the increased use of bread among the lower income urban
born, which may have negative consequences due to its higher cost than
tortillas; use of bread may also reflect high cost or lack of availability of
firewood and lack of fuel, along with prestige issues, may account for the
lack of use among those born in the city of *caldos* at mid-day, in favor of
faster cooking *sopas*. In any case, the rural *caldo*-eaters retain the advantage in food consumption.

Another difference in food consumption is the allocation of the food budget. Those born in the city of lower incomes have the lowest consumption of all food types (except meat and dairy, both of which are relatively expensive). Arroyo Lindo lower income households use a lesser amount of dairy products, and at least some of this is home produced. Therefore, those born in the city of lower incomes are spending more money on dairy products than are those of similar income levels who live in the rural areas. Those born in the city of lower incomes also use 42% more meat than do those in Arroyo Lindo – therefore they are spending a higher percentage of their food budget on meat. We can consider this expense to come out of the food budget, as the meat is largely consumed at home. If it were eaten out, it might be coming from a different area of the household budget; it is mostly the men who eat out and do so while socializing with friends. Nutritional education might therefore be appropriate. The only problem is that doing so would be going against the local sense of prestige. Meat is a food of very high prestige value; it would be an uphill battle to decrease meat consumption in any part of Sonora.

Another difference between the lower income rural and urban born households may be the extent to which the wives are economically active. Others have reported difficulty in getting reliable information on women's economic activity (Whiteford 1982), although in Chile "migrant women displayed a surprising degree of participation in the labor force" (Herrick 1965:88). I will nonetheless presume that the pattern suggested by my sample is correct. Therefore, part of the greater nutritional problem in the urban areas may be that the lower income urban households that were sampled by Valencia (1981) were in large part made up of rural born husbands and urban born wives who are less frequently economically active. As we have seen, the presence of an economically active wife has a positive effect on dietary intakes, especially at the lower available income levels, the population we would expect to be at the greatest nutritional risk. Another factor to consider is the extent to which Valencia's (1981) urban households were headed by women. Such households were not a part of the present study, and Logan (1981) suggests that they are likely to be poorer.

In summary, the greater nutritional problems in the urban areas are probably due to a combination of factors, including less home production, different types of foods being used, and less economic activity among wives. The present generation of migrants is not at nutritional risk, although rural to urban migration in Sonora may lead to greater nutritional problems in the urban areas – but only for those of the second generation for whom economic mobility has not been possible.

Possible but impractical recommendations for improving the nutritional situation in the urban areas include subsidizing water rates, which would increase home production of food, but would be very expensive – the middle class would use the water on lawns – and would not make ecological sense. Nutrition education with respect to decreasing the percentage of the food budget used for meat would run counter to existing prestige values.

A change that might be more feasible would be to encourage lower income households to keep chickens, which could be largely the responsibility of the children; the programs could be advocated through the schools. Subsidized cooking gas rates might also be considered, as this might encourage increased use by the lower income urban born of foods that require longer cooking, such as *caldos*. Finally, new employment opportunities could be targeted either at adult men or women, not their teen-aged children; solving the employment problems of young adults may have little short range impact on improving nutritional status. However, we should note that the wives in this sample who improve their families' nutritional status by their economic activity may do so because the types of work they do are largely part-time; therefore, there is no conflict with childcare. Jobs created for adult women should either provide childcare, or have flexible hours and/or the possibility of part-time employment. Further, if producing improved nutritional status is considered as an aspect of overall production, it may be necessary to re-assess the role of the informal sector of the economy – the sector in which women often prefer to work due to the flexibility and control over hours that they retain, eliminating potential conflicts with childcare.

Factors Affecting Malnutrition Among School Age Children and Females

As discussed in the sections on intra-household distribution, differential access to food by older age groups does not seem to be strongly correlated with the nutritional problems of school-age children. Other factors that affect consumption by school-age children of foods in the MISC category may be involved. School-age children in general have very high rates of consumption of these high energy, low nutrient foods. However, consumption of these items decreases under many circumstances: it is lowest at the lowest household incomes, among those born in the city, and in multiple worker households. And at lower available incomes, male consumption of MISC exceeds that of females.

While not the most nutritionally sound approach, and certainly not the most efficient way of maximizing calories/peso, increased household expenditures on MISC do represent the most direct way of getting increased calories directed to school-age children, as opposed to other members of the household. The frequency with which school-age children fall into a household type which is likely to have reduced consumption of MISC – i.e., urban, those of the very lowest household incomes, or a multiple worker household – may explain the clustering of nutritional problems in this age group. The risk of female school-aged children in households of these types would be even greater. Here then, is a situation, that poses a tremendous challenge for the nutrition educator.

Another way of creating an equally high calorie input would be through increased use of shortening and oil, but consumption of these foods does not go as directly to the school-age children. Much increased household consumption of dairy and fruit would go to pre-school and school-age children; however, the calorie value of these foods is lower then that of MISC. It is therefore necessary to encourage the use of some sort of snack food of high caloric value, but of greater nutrient density and lower cost than that of foods in the MISC group. Food scientists interested in this problem could be asked to try to develop a low cost snack using for example, peanuts and red chile as a base (red chile snacks are a favorite of Sonoran children). In many schools, the snack foods available at recess are chosen by the teachers. A nutrition education program aimed at changing the kinds of snacks the teachers make available would be an efficient way to attack this problem.

The policy of the Mexican government in the 1980's was to reduce food subsidies, but if any are to be re-instated, it would be best to include subsidies on foods that would be likely to have the greatest effects on dietary adequacy. Subsidizing foods that represent the staples of lower income households would have the effects of increasing the available incomes of these households. For Sonora, these foods include eggs, vegetable shortening and/or cooking oil, beans, and white flour. Greater amounts of oil and shortening are used in cooking by lower income households and therefore provide an important source of calories. Lower income households generally buy flour and make their own tortillas, while the higher income groups purchase tortillas and/or use bread, and consume less grains in general. Beans are used more by lower income households than they are by households of higher income levels. Finally, although egg consumption is highest in the middle income groups, lower prices would probably increase use of eggs among households in lower income households.

CONCLUSIONS

This study has illustrated the specific ways in which an anthropologist can contribute to the study and understanding of the dietary intake component of nutritional problems. As the foci and research techniques of the anthropologist are different from those of other disciplines, the types of research questions that can be usefully addressed by anthropological investigation also differ.

The concern of the anthropologist is behavior, and especially the context in which the behavior takes place. As discussed above, the context of a household's income may affect the extent to which total household income does not equal the amount of income available for household expenses (including the purchasing of food). It also effects the ways in which available income is spent. This combination of factors will result in different dietary and nutritional outcomes at similar total household income levels. Also of importance to the anthropologist is the extent to which beliefs (such as traditional food beliefs) actually affect behavior.

A role for the anthropologist in the planning and implementation of development policies and programs might be to identify, prior to the design of the intervention program, the social and cultural variables which have the greatest effects on available income in the particular area for which the program is being planned (unless the program is planned for a part of the world where multiple worker households are rare). Programs could then be designed to focus on manipulation of the variable(s) which will have the greatest impact. Using available income as an outcome measure is also a means by which the effectiveness of programs and policies can be easily evaluated. This approach sees food policy as going beyond manipulation of food prices. As the interventions suggested in the Sonoran case indicate, food policy is viewed as part of an overall approach to development which includes improved nutritional status as one of its goals.

I have throughout the manuscript refrained from taking advantage of hindsight in evaluating the patterns and problems observed in Sonora in the 1980's. Yet to do so provides an excellent example of the application of the model of analysis demonstrated in this book. The nutritional and land situations in the early 1980's, particularly in Arroyo Lindo, were unlike that much of northern Mexico, but in many ways more similar to areas of Mexico, such as Chiapas in southern Mexico, the scene of considerable contemporary unrest. As such, current government policies can be evaluated in terms of their likely nutritional impact, both in the region studied, and possibly in other areas of Mexico as well.

With specific reference to the recommendations suggested based on the data collected in the early 1980's, the direction the Mexican government has taken in recent years appears to be the exact opposite of those recommendations. Government subsidies on food have been reduced, or eliminated. Issues of rural development and more equitable distribution of land have been largely dismissed, as *ejidos* are now permitted to become privatized. These latter changes may not be entirely negative. Will sales of *ejido* land result in more small holders in villages like Arroyo Lindo, or will the land just fall back into the hands of large owners such as the Perez family? *Ejido* land owners from Arroyo Lindo who can sell their lands may have more resources available to enable them to move to the cities, and/or start small businesses in the village. It is possible that if rural people are able to make a living in ways that do not depend on land and cattle, some of the land problems may reduce in intensity.

But the changes in other sectors of the society look less promising. NAFTA will make Mexican small family businesses and work in the informal sector very vulnerable to competition with large multinational corporations. Will past and present migrants to the city lose their small businesses? Will it become more difficult for women to operate small money making ventures? If the move is from small business employment to working for large corporations which treat workers as do the *macquiladoras* which have proliferated along the U.S.–Mexico border, then the outlook is dismal indeed. Analysis of data from studies such as those of Fernandez-Kelly (1983) suggest that the impact of such a change will be a drastic drop in household available income.

Thus, the baseline data which this study provides strongly imply that the overall nutritional impact of such policies will be negative. Mexico seeks to join the ranks of the fully industrialized countries of the world. But rather than becoming more like the countries of the world which have largely freed their populations from malnutrition, current Mexican government policies may be in the process of accomplishing the exact opposite. The data presented here suggest that recent policy changes will not result in the Mexican population joining others at a well-laden dining table. To the contrary, the vulnerable segments of the Mexican population may not only find that they have remained in the kitchen, and but also discover that their only move has been out of the frying pan and into the fire.

APPENDIX A: DIETARY DATA COLLECTION FORMS

Household Food Use

Day _____

Recipes

Name of Meal	*Name of Dish*	*Ingredients*	*Amounts*

Individual Consumption

Name _____

Day _____

Key

Question 2 – Name of meal

1 Breakfast
2 Brunch
3 Lunch
4 Dinner
5 Supper
6 Coffee (beverage) break
7 Snack
8 Other

Question 3 – With whom did you eat

1 Alone
2 With other household member(s)
3 With non-household member(s)
4 With both household and non-household member(s)

Q1 Time	Q2 Name of meal	Q3 With whom	Q4 Food/Drink	Amount	Household Supply		
					Eaten Home	Eaten Out	No – Where?

Was your food/drink consumption on this day typical of what you usually eat/drink on this day of the week?

Yes	1
No	2

If *no*, why is it different?

Ill	1
Short of Cash	2
Traveling	3
Social occasion	4
Holiday	5
Not enough time to eat	6
Other (explain) _____	7

_____

_____

As of now, how would you describe your health?

Excellent	1
Good	2
Fair	3
Poor	4

APPENDIX B

ETHNOGRAPHIC INTERVIEW FORM

Household ID# _____

Date: _____ Time: _____

1. (a) Who are the members of this household?
   (b) What are their ages?
   (c) In school?
   (d) If employed, how many hours/week?
   (e) How is each related to the head of household?

	a. First name	b. Age	c. In school	d. Employed hrs/wk	e. Relationship
1.					
2.					
3.					
4.					
5.					
6.					
7.					
8.					
9.					

2. What kind of work does the husband do? _____
   What kinds of physical activity does this involve?

3. What kind of work does the wife do? _____
   What kinds of physical activity does this involve?

4. What is his highest grade of formal schooling?_____

5. What is her highest grade of formal schooling?_____

6. How often does someone do a major food shopping?
   More than once a week   1–1
   Once a week   1–2
   Once every two weeks   1–3
   Once a month or less   1–4
   Never   1–5

7. What kind of store?
   Supermarket
   Small grocery store (includes village store)

Quick market (includes tiendas)
Food co-op
Other (includes market)
Specialty stores

8. Is milk for the family:
   Purchased in a store   1
   Delivered   2
   Not purchased   3
   Don't know   4
   Other   5

9. What do you consider your ethnic background to be?

10. Do you have a:

	YES	NO
Vegetable garden	1	0
Fruit tree	1	0
Chickens	1	0
Dogs, cats	1	0
Cattle	1	0

11. What language do you speak in your house?

12. Do you have relatives in Arroyo Lindo? This neighborhood?
    Hermosillo? Tucson?

13. Neighborhood (colonia) of household _____

14. (a) Do you send money to relatives in Hermosillo? Arroyo Lindo?
        Other relatives
    (b) Do you receive money from relatives in Hermosillo? Arroyo
        Lindo? Other relatives?

15. Does your family eat many casseroles or one-pot meals? Why?
    Which ones?

16. What is the non-U.S./Mexican ancestry for each adult? (Since 1900
    give approximate immigration date; before that use 1/2 century).
    For adult heads of household, which generation born in U.S./Mexico
    are they? (1st, 2nd, etc.)

17. How do you think this ethnic background affects your food
    consumption?

18. What was your home region in the U.S./Mexico prior to moving to
    Hermosillo?
    How does this affect your eating patterns?

19. How long have you lived in this neighborhood?
    How long in Hermosillo?
    How long in Sonora?

20. How has moving to Hermosillo affected food consumption?
    Do you buy any food in the U.S.?
    What kinds? When? Why?

21. Do you change your eating patterns with the seasons? How?

22. Do you eat as your parents did (do)?
    How SAME?
    How DIFFERENT?

23. How often do you use cookbooks as opposed to family recipes for dinner?
    How often does your mother use cookbooks as opposed to family recipes?
    How many cookbooks do you own?

24. Do you have any special bowls or utensils for preparing ethnic dishes? (e.g. tortilla press, wok, chopping bowls, etc.)
    Do you own any other items which you think indicate ethnic identity? If so, what?

25. a) Do you ever try new foods or new recipes?
       If so, where do you get the ideas?
       What kinds of foods? For which meals?
       Which days of the week or year?
    b) Do your kids or husband ever ask you to try new foods?
       Where do they get the ideas?
       What kinds of things?
       Which meals?
    c) How do the likes and dislikes of your husband affect what your family eats?
       The likes and dislikes of your children?
       Of other household members?
       Your own preferences?

26. a) What does your family eat on:
       Thanksgiving?
       Christmas/Easter?
    b) What other special ethnic or religious days does family celebrate?
       What foods are eaten?
    c) What foods would be served to house guests?
       What foods would be served for a dinner party?
       What foods would be served for a wedding?
    d) What are special foods for when household members are sick or just recuperating?
       Do you celebrate birthdays?
       What kinds of foods do you eat?

e) Is food ever used (given or received) as a gift? When? To Whom?
What kinds of food are appropriate?
What does this mean compared to other kinds of gifts?

27. a) How do you know that you have prepared enough food?
    b) What do you consider to be "leftovers"?
    c) Of food prepared but not eaten, how do you decide to store vs. throw out?
       Discard from storage?
    d) Is it a sign of politeness to not finish the last bit of food in a serving bowl or on your plate when you are eating at someone else's house?
    e) How is food in your house served?
    f) Is it okay to leave food on your plate at home? When is it okay to "waste" food?

28. Do you have special feelings associated with any particular foods? Which ones? What? Why?
    How does this affect your use of these foods?

29. Do you use the term "junk food"? What do you mean by it? What foods are included in the category?
    Why are these foods classified as "junk foods"?
    (if not mentioned, is fast food junk food?)
    Do you or your family ever eat them? Which ones?

30. Do you use the term "health food"? What do you mean by it? What foods are included in the category?
    Why are these foods classified as "health foods"?
    Do you or your family ever eat them? Which ones?
    Is there a difference between health foods and healthy foods? If so, explain.
    Is there a relationship between what kinds of foods a person eats and how his/her state of health is? (if yes) what kinds of foods should you eat to stay in good health?

31. What do you consider to be "American Food"?
    Why? Do you eat it? How often? Are there any aspects of American food which you dislike? Be specific.

32. a) What do you consider to be Mexican food?
       Why? Do you eat it? How often?
       Are there any aspects of Mexican food
       which you dislike? Be specific.
    b) Are there any foods you should eat or avoid when you are pregnant? Why?

    c) Are there any foods you should eat or avoid when you are nursing?
       Why?

    d) If it is very hot out and you have been in the sun, are there any
       beverages you should drink, or avoid drinking? Why?

    e) Are there any foods which should not be eaten together? Why?
       What about watermelon and milk?

33. a) What do you think the rich eat?

    b) What do you think the poor eat?

34. Indicate whether this household has the following items, and if appropriate, how many:

    a. telephone (working) (#)
    b. dishwasher
    c. washer
    d. dryer
    e. freezer (in refrig. or separate?)
    f. refrigerator (#)
    g. microwave oven
    h. electricity
    i. sink
    j. oven (type: gas, electric, wood)
    k. range (type)
    l. blender
    m. food processor
    n. TV (color or black/white, #)
    o. stereo
    p. car (#, other comments)
    q. crockpot
    r. other important? Specify.
    s. cement floor
    t. dirt floor
    u. indoor bathroom
    v. latrine
    w. no bathroom
    x. water in the house
    y. water in the yard
    z. number of rooms in house

35. Are any of the above currently not working?
    If so, how long have they not been working?

36. Do any of the above affect how you buy or cook? (If any are out of order, has this affected buying or cooking?)

37. What would you most like to have that you don't? Why?

Under what circumstances might you get it?
38. Has inflation caused changes in your lifestyle?
In what areas? (food purchases, travel, work, services, recreation)
If not, why?
39. How much does each person who works earn?
How much does each person who works give to the husband or wife?

References

Anderson, E. N. Jr. and M. L. Anderson (1977) Modern China: South. In *Food in Chinese Culture*. K. C. Chang, ed. Yale University Press, New Haven, pp. 317–382.

Arizpe, Lourdes (1977) Women in the Informal Labor Sector: The Case of Mexico City. *Signs* 3, pp. 25–37.

Arizpe, Lourdes (1981) The Rural Exodus in Mexico and Mexican Migration to the United States. *International Migration Review* Vol. 15, No. 4, pp. 626–649.

AuCoin, Dale, M. Haley, J. Rae, and M. Cole (1972) A Comparative Study of Food Habits: Influence of Age, Sex and Selected Family Characteristics. *Canadian Journal of Public Health* 63:143–157.

Barkin, David (1975) Regional Development and Interregional Equity: A Mexican Case Study. In *Urbanization and Inequality*. Wayne A. Cornelius and Felicity M. Trueblood, eds. Sage Publications, Beverly Hills, pp. 277–299.

Becker, Gary (1981) *A Treatise on the Family*. Harvard University Press, Cambridge, Mass.

Beneria, Lourdes and Martha Roldan (1987) *The Crossroads of Class and Gender*. The University of Chicago Press, Chicago.

Bennett, J. W., K. L. Smith and H. Passin (1942) Food and Culture in Southern Illinois – A Preliminary Report. *American Sociological Review* 7:645–60.

Berg, Alan (1972) Industry's Struggle with World Malnutrition. *Harvard Business Review* 50, (January–February) pp. 130–141.

Berg, Alan (1973) *The Nutrition Factor*. The Brookings Institution, Washington, D.C.

Black, Susan J. and Diva Sanjur (1980) Nutrition in Rio Piedros: A Study of Internal Migration and Maternal Diets. *Ecology of Food and Nutrition* Vol. 10, pp. 25–33.

Bradfield, Stillman (1973) Selectivity in Rural–Urban Migration: The Case of Huaylas, Peru. In *Urban Anthropology*. A. Southhall, ed. Oxford University Press, London, pp. 351–372.

Burgess, Anne and R. F. A. Dean (1962) *Malnutrition and Food Habits*. Tavistock Publications, London.

Butterworth, D. S. (1962) A Study of the Urbanization Process Among Mixtec Migrants from Tilantongo in Mexico City. *America Indigena* 22 pp. 257–74.

Carvajal, Manuel and David Geithman (1974) An Economic Analysis of Migration in Costa Rica. *Economic Development and Cultural Change* Vol. 23, No. 1, pp. 105–122.

Chadhury, R. (1984) Determinants of Dietary Intake and Dietary Adequacy for Pre-School Children in Bangladesh. *Food and Nutrition Bulletin.* Vol. 6, No. 4, pp. 24–33.

Chavez, Miriam *et al.* (1976) The Epidemiology of Good Nutrition in a Population with a High Prevalence of Malnutrition. In *La Desnutricion y La Salud en Mexico.* Carlos Perez and Adolfo Chavez, eds. Division de Nutricion, Instituto Nacional De La Nutricion. Publicacion L–34. Tlalpan, Mexico, D.F.

Clark, M. (1959) *Health in the Mexican-American Culture.* University of California Press, Berkeley.

Cussler, Margaret T. and M. L. de Give (1942) The Effect of Human Relations on Food Habits in the Rural Southeast. *Applied Anthropology* 1(3):13–18.

den Hartog, A. P. and A. Bornstein-Johanssen (1976) Social Science, Food, and Nutrition. In *Development from Below: Anthropologists and Development Situations.* D. C. Pitt, ed. Mouton Publications, The Hague, pp. 97–123.

Devadas, R. P. (1970) Social and Cultural Factors Influencing Malnutrition. *Journal of Home Economics* 62:164–171.

Dewalt, Kathleen M. and Gretel H. Pelto (1976) Food Use and Household Ecology in a Mexican Community. In *Nutrition and Anthropology in Action.* Thomas K. Fitzgerald, ed. Van Gorcum. Assen. pp. 79–93.

Dewalt, K. M., P. B. Kelley and G. H. Pelto (1980) Nutritional Correlates of Economic Microdifferentiation in a Highland Mexican Community. In *Nutritional Anthropology.* N. W. Jerome, R. F. Kandel, and G. H. Pelto, eds. Redgrave Publishing Company, Pleasantville, New York, pp. 205–221.

Dwyer, Daisy Hilse (1983) *Women and Income in the Third World: Implications for Policy.* Working Paper No. 18. The Population Council, New York.

Erasmus, Charles J. (1961) *Man Takes Control.* University of Minnesota Press, Minneapolis.

Estado de Sonora (1980) *X Censo General de Poblacion y Vivienda: Resultados Preliminares.* December. Mexico, D.F.

Fapohunda, Eleanor (1988) The Nonpooling Household: A Challenge to Theory. In *A Home Divided* D. Dwyer and J. Bruce, eds. Stanford University, Press, Stanford, pp. 143–154.

Fernandez-Kelley, María Patricia (1983) Maquiladora Work and Household Organization: An Ethnographic Account. In *For We Are Sold, I and My People: Women and Industry in Mexico's Frontier.* State University Press of New York, Albany, pp. 151–194.

Fitzgerald, T. K. (1976) Ipomoea Batatas: The Sweet Potato Revisited. *Ecology of Food and Nutrition* 5:107–14.

Fleuret, P. and A. Fleuret (1980) Nutrition, Consumption, and Agricultural Change. *Human Organization* 39(3):250–260.

Fleuret, Patrick and Ann Fleuret (1983) Socio-Economic Determinants of Child Nutrition in Taita, Kenya: A Call for Discussion. *Culture and Agriculture* Issue 19, pp. 8–20.

Fleuret, Patrick and Fleuret, A. (1991) Social Organization, Resource Management, and Child Nutrition in the Taita Hills, Kenya. *American Anthropologist* Vol. 93, No. 1, pp. 91–114.

Gittinger, J., Leslie J. and Hoisington, C., eds. (1987) *Food Policy*. Johns Hopkins University Press, Baltimore.

Graedon, Teresa L. Frost (1976) Health and Nutritional Status in an Urban Community of Southern Mexico. Unpublished doctoral dissertation, University of Michigan.

Gray, Cheryl Williamson (1982) *Food Consumption Parameters for Brazil and their Application to Food Policy*. Research Report 32. International Food Policy Research Institute, Washington, D.C.

Greiner, Ted and Michael C. Latham (1981) Factors Associated with Nutritional Status Among Young Children in St. Vincent. *Ecology of Food and Nutrition*, Vol. 10, pp. 135–141.

Gross, D. R. and B. Underwood (1971) Technological Change and Calorie Costs: Sisal Agriculture in Northeastern Brazil. *American Anthropologist* 73(31):725–740.

Guyer, Jane J. (1980) *Household Budgets and Women's Incomes*. Working Paper No. 28. African Studies Center. Boston University, Brookline.

Hamil, P., T. Drizd, C. Johnson, R. Reed, A. Roche and W. Moore (1979) Physical Growth: National Center for Health Statistics Percentiles. *American Journal of clinical Nutrition* 32:607–629.

Herrick, Bruce (1965) *Urban Migration and Economic Development in Chile*. The MIT Press, Cambridge.

Hewes, Leslie (1935) Huepac: An Agricultural Village of Sonora, Mexico. *Economic Geography*, Vol. 11, No. 3, pp. 284–92.

Immink, Maarten D. C., D. Sanjur, and M. Burgos (1983) Nutritional Consequences of United States Migration Patterns among Puerto Rican Women. *Ecology of Food and Nutrition* Vol. 13, pp. 139–148.

Kemp, W. B. (1971) The Flow of Energy in a Hunting Society. *Scientific American* 225(3):104–115.

Kemper, Robert V. (1981) Obstacles and Opportunities: Household Economics in Tzintzuntzan Migrants in Mexico City. *Urban Anthropology* Vol. 10, Number 3, Fall, pp. 211–119.

Kumar, Shubh K. (1978) *Role of the Household Economy in Child Nutrition at Low Income.* Occasional Paper No. 95. Department of Agricultural Economics, Cornell University, Ithaca.

Laderman, Carol (1983) *Wives and Midwives.* University of California Press, Berkeley.

Leininger, Madeline M. (1970) Some Cross-Cultural Universal and Non-Universal Functions, Beliefs, and Practices of Food. In *Dimensions of Nutrition.* Jacqueline Dupont, ed. Colorado Associated University Press, Boulder, pp. 153–179.

LERES (Liga de Economistas Revolucionarios del Estado de Sonora, a.c.) (1979) Monográficas de los 69 Municipios que Integran el Estado de Sonora. Hermosillo, Sonora. Typescript.

Lewis, Oscar (1951) *Life in a Mexican Village: Tepoztlan Restudied.* University of Illinois Press, Urbana.

Logan, Kathleen (1981) Getting By with Less: Economic Strategies of Lower Income Households in Guadalajaura. *Urban Anthropology,* Vol. 10, Number 3, Fall, pp. 231–246.

Marchione, T. J. (1980) Factors Associated with Malnutrition in the children of Western Jamaica. In *Nutritional Anthropology.* N. W. Jerome, R. F. Kandel and G. H. Pelto, eds. Redgrave Publishing Company, Pleasantville, N.Y., pp. 223–273.

McKenzie, J. C. (1974) The Impact of Economic and Social Status on Food Choice. *Proceedings of the Nutrition Society* 33:67–73.

Messer, Ellen (1976) The Ecology of Vegetarian Diet in a Modernizing Mexican Community. In *Nutrition and Anthropology in Action.* Thomas K. Fitzgerald ed. Van Gorcum, Assen., pp. 117–124.

Michigan Department of Public Health (1980) *Basic Nutrition Facts.* Michigan Department of Public Health, Lansing.

Morrison, Peter A. (1977) The Functions and Dynamics of the Migration Process. In *Internal Migration.* Alan A. Brown and Egon Neuberger, eds. Academic Press, New York, pp. 61–72.

Nalbandian, Anahid, James G. Bergan, and Phyllis T. Brown (1981) Three Generations of Armenians: Food Habits and Dietary Status. *Journal of the American Dietetic Association,* Vol. 79, pp. 694–699.

Owen, Roger C. (1959) *Marobavi: A Study of an Assimilated Group in Northern Sonora.* Anthropological Papers of the University of Arizona, Number 3, Tucson.

Perlman, Janice E. (1976) *The Myth of Marginality.* University of California Press, Berkeley.

Pinstrup-Andersen, Per (1981) Food Policy, Household Behavior and Nutrition. Paper presented to the Agricultural Economics Society of Southeast Asia, Singapore, November 3–7, 1981.

Pinstrup-Andersen, Per (1983) Estimating the Nutritional Impact of Food Policies: A Note on the Analytical Approach. Paper presented at the XI International Congress of the International Union of Anthropological and Ethnological Sciences. Vancouver, August 20–25.

Popkin, B. M. and F. S. Solon (1976) Income, Time, The Working Mother and Child Nutriture. *Journal of Tropical Pediatrics and Environmental Child Health* 22:156–166.

Preston, David A. (1969) Rural Emigration in Andean America. *Human Organization*, Vol. 28, No. 4, pp. 279–286.

Ramos Galvan, Rafael (1975) *Archivos de Investigacion Medica. Somatometria Pediatrica*, No. 6, Sup. 1, Ediciones Culturales Mexicana, S. A. Mexico, pp. 312–390.

Read, Margaret (1964) The Role of the Anthropologist. In *Changing Food Habits*, John Yudkin and J. C. McKenzie, eds. MacGibbon and Kee, London, pp. 46–61.

Roberts, Byran (1973) *Organizing Strangers*. University of Texas Press, Austin.

Roldan, Martha (1988) Renegotiating the Marriage Contract: Intrahousehold Patterns of Money Allocation and Women's Subordination Among Domestic Outworkers in Mexico City. In *A Home Divided*, D. Dwyer and J. Bruce, eds. Stanford University Press, Stanford, pp. 229–247.

Salaff, Janet (1981) Singapore Women. In *Women and World Change*. Naomi Black and Ann Baker Cottrell, eds. Sage Publications, Beverly Hills, pp. 57–82.

Sanderson, Steven E. (1981) *Agrarian Populism and the Mexican State*. University of California, Berkeley.

Shadow, Robert D. (1979) Differential Out-Migration: A Comparison of Internal and International Migration from Villa Guerrero, Jalisco (Mexico). In *Migration Across Frontiers: Mexico and the United States*, Fernando Camara and Robert V. Kemper, eds. Institute for Mesoamerican studies, University of New York at Albany, pp. 67–83.

Sheridan, Thomas (1983) Where the Dove Calls: Economic Inequality and Agrarian Conflict in the Municipio of Cucurpe, Sonora. Unpublished doctoral dissertation, University of Arizona.

Silvers, Arthur and Pierre Crossen (1980) *Rural Development and Urban-Bound Migration in Mexico*. Resources for the Future, Research Paper R-17, Washington, D.C.

Simic, Andrei (1973) *The Peasant-Urbanites: A Study of Rural–Urban Migration in Serbia*. Seminar Press, New York.

Simmons, Alan B. and Ramiro Cardona (1972) Rural–Urban Migration: Who Comes, Who Stays, Who Returns? The Case of Bogota, Columbia, 1929–1968. *International Migration Review.* Vol. 6, pp. 166–181.

Smith, Meredith E., Steven K. Paulsen, William Fougere and S. J. Ritchey (1983) Socioeconomic, Education and Health Factors Influencing Growth of Rural Haitian Children. *Ecology of Food and Nutrition*, Vol. 13, pp. 99–108.

Soto Federico, Lauro (1982) Arroyo Lindo, Sonora-Estudio de la Comunidad. Typescript. Available in files of Centro de Salud, Hermosillo.

Sub' Secretaría de Ganadería (1981) Censo de Poblacion de Ganado en el Año 1981. Secretaría de Fomento Agropecuario, Gobierno de Estado de Sonora, Hermosillo. Typescript.

Timmer, C., Falcon, W. and S. Pearson (1983) *Food Policy Analysis.* Johns Hopkins University Press, Baltimore.

Tripp, Robert B. (1982) Farmers and Traders: Some Economic Determinants of Nutritional Status in Northern Ghana. *Food and Nutrition Bulletin*, Vol. 8, No. 1, pp. 3–11.

Valencia, Mauro (1980) Estudio Nutricional en la Zona Serrana del Estado de Sonora. Instituto de Investigaciones y Estudios Superiores del Noroeste, A. C. Hermosillo, Sonora. Typescript.

Valencia, Mauro E. (1981) Estudio Nutritional en Centros Urbanos Marginados de Sonora. Instituto de Investigacion y Estudios Superiores de Noroeste, A. C. Hermosillo, Sonora. Typescript.

Whiteford, M. (1982) The Interface of Cultural Factors with Nutritional Well Being. *Medical Anthropology* 6(4): 221–230.

Whitehead, Ann (1981) "I'm Hungry, Mum": The Politics of Domestic Budgeting. In *Of Marriage and the Market*, Kate Young, Carol Wolkowitz and Roslyn McCullagh, eds. CSE Books, London.

Wray, Joe D. and Alfredo Aguirre (1969) Protein-Calorie Malnutrition in Candelaria, Colombia. *Journal of Tropical Pediatrics*, Vol. 15, pp. 76–98.